WHAT OTHERS ARE SAYING ABOUT
The Parent Trapped Within

Scenes of grownups behaving badly at kids' sporting events have become all too familiar. You've undoubtedly heard about more than a few, whether you've witnessed them in person, read about them in the news or watched them on viral videos. You've also, almost certainly, said to yourself, "Wow, I'd never do that at my kid's game."

But would you?

We all want to be supportive parents, and we all want the best for our children. But if an obviously bad call doesn't go our way, or if a parent of someone from the opposing team starts getting overly vocal, could we keep our cool?

In this book, Dave Vilhauer explores the challenges of being a good sports parent and offers sound advice on how to avoid crossing the line. His work features plenty of anecdotes, some from his personal experience as a parent and some he collected during his decades-long career as a member of the sports media. Though most of the stories are set in his—and for a time my—home state of South Dakota, there is a universality to them that any parent or athlete can relate to. If enough people heed his advice, youth and high school athletics can get back to being what they're supposed to be, fun experiences for young people as they learn life lessons about teamwork and sportsmanship.

—*Eddie Timanus*, USA Today

D1545162

Wow, what a great book! Dave has really captured the meaning of *The Parent Trapped Within*. This book is a very relaxed read, filled with many realistic, down to earth, truthful stories of many "parents trapped within." As much as I hate to admit it, I found myself, repeatedly, one of those "parents trapped within."

I think everyone who reads this book will be able to relate to the detailed events that Dave shares throughout his many reports and experiences as a journalist and more importantly, a dad. I love his parental incite and the significant stories he shares in this book. He has experienced so much through his children and his career, giving him substantial expertise on this subject matter. I appreciate the quotes that he used from honorable coaches to highlight each chapter of the book.

Throughout our children's athletic careers and beyond, may we all reflect on the material in this book and treasure the life lessons handed to us as we watch children participate in athletic contests. May we all learn to enjoy the journey and be the parent or fan that these young athletes deserve to have cheering them on in the stands. Lastly, may we appreciate their efforts and experiences and be proud of every moment in these young people's lives. Enjoy the book, I certainly did!

—*Jo Auch*, Assistant Executive Director,
South Dakota High School Activities Association

Being an athlete, a parent of athletes, and a coach has allowed me to see sports from a variety of different perspectives. This is a book I wish I would have read years ago. It made me realize that perhaps I was "one of those parents," and I wish I would have had more insight into what was truly important while my kids were competing.

Dave's stories made me think and his insight from a reporter's angle was extremely valuable. Every coach, parent, and athlete needs to read this book! It will teach you the value of sports, more specifically how to make sure you're being the right type of parent to your athlete!

—*Holly Hoffman*, Professional Speaker and Author

The Parent Trapped Within (A Guide to Sports Parenting) is an easy-to-read guide to being the best sports parent you can be. Dave Vilhauer writes with a smooth style that doesn't talk down to parents and uses real-world examples to accurately illustrate his points. This is a must-read for every parent who has a child playing sports."

—*Dave Goren*, Executive Director, National Sports Media Association
Adjunct Faculty—Wake Forest University - Fall 2017
Sideline Reporter—Wake Forest IMG Sports Network
Director—Atlantic Coast Sports Media Association

THE PARENT
TRAPPED WITHIN

A GUIDE TO
SPORTS PARENTING

DAVE VILHAUER

BASELINE PUBLISHING

The Parent Trapped Within
Dave Vilhauer

© 2019 Baseline Publishing

ISBN 978-0-578-21779-6

Cover design and interior layout by Five J's Design | *fivejsdesign.com*

TABLE OF CONTENTS

INTRODUCTION

Thank you for taking time to read this copy of *The Parent Trapped Within*. There are so many things you could be doing right now and I am honored that you chose to do this. I hope that you will find this book well worth your time.

The information contained in this book is designed to provide insight into what sports has become in our society and what I believe the roles of parents should be in that environment.

The Parent Trapped Within is not a shot at all sports parents everywhere. In fact, without parents of athletes, it's safe to say there probably wouldn't be sports. I appreciate all of the hours of sacrifice that parents make for their athletes, the hours spent in vehicles, the time spent washing uniforms, the money spent buying equipment. That does not even include all of the effort spent teaching children the basics of the game.

What *The Parent Trapped Within* is intended to be, is an inside look at my own personal experiences as a nearly 40-year member of the media and a parent of an athlete. The aim of this book is to shed light on the difficulties of being a sports parent. How do parents find the right balance between supporting their children without crossing the line and providing unsolicited and unwanted coaching advice? How do parents react when they feel their athletes aren't getting fair calls from officials? How do parents find the answer to the question: what is the definition of success?

Please keep in mind that for the most part this book references those who are parents of high school athletes or younger. College athletics are much different in the fact that many of those participants are on scholarship and are among the very few gifted enough to compete at the next level. While many of the same principles of parenting are still applicable, the atmosphere is much different surrounding college sports compared to high school.

As word has spread that I am writing a book on sports parenting, it has been interesting to see how many people have shared a story or two of their own experiences. If you are around sports at all these days, chances are you too have witnessed examples of unacceptable parental behavior.

I would like to believe that most parents have the best of intentions at heart. The problem is, once those parents become part of the process, those intentions are often overtaken by the spirit of competition. Soon judgments are clouded, emotions become raw and reputations are placed at risk.

The title of this book really has multiple meanings. First, it speaks to parents who might feel trapped, wanting to provide support to their favorite athlete, yet afraid of saying the wrong thing. Second, the parent trapped within, also encompasses all parents who are well intentioned, but suddenly find themselves trapped in the system of athletics, unable to control their emotions during the heat of competition.

I have a hunch that sports parents are a much more serious issue in our culture than I even realize. Not that this book will supply definitive solutions to all of the problems associated with sports parenting. But I'm hoping that it might provide useful information for coaches and parents alike on ways to avoid potential issues or deal with them when they arise.

In writing vernacular, I am now moving on to a new chapter of my life. I am no longer a sports parent and I'm not sure it will totally hit me until future seasons roll around. However, I have been around sports my entire life and I don't see that changing any time soon. I love athletics and all of the life lessons they have to offer. I also cherish the many life-long friendships that I feel blessed to have cultivated through athletics. And I'm grateful that sports have provided me with many memories, some of which you will discover in the pages ahead.

Again, thank you for taking time to read *The Parent Trapped Within*. I believe that there are stories that will make you laugh, I think that there are some that will make you sad, but above all, I hope that you will find parts that will make you think.

It is my desire that this book will not be all about me or my family members, and while there will be many references to coaches and players from all across South Dakota, that in the end it will not be about them, either. My goal is that *The Parent Trapped Within* will be much like sports itself in that in some small way it will bring individuals together and help them to understand that they are truly a part of something much bigger and better than themselves.

FOREWORD

On Father's Day a few years ago, we had the Los Angeles Angels on our Sunday Night Baseball broadcast, and before that game, I fished around for some anecdotes about sons and dads to tell on air. Mike Trout's father played in the minor leagues for a time and had been a really good professional hitter, and after he finished a round of batting practice, I intercepted him outside the cage to ask about his Dad's role in his progress as the best player on the planet.

"How much input does your father give you on your hitting?" I asked.

"We don't really talk about hitting," he said.

The answer surprised me. Especially because I'd seen so many parents mentor their sons closely, hovering—especially in cases when the Dad had played. "I'm sure he knows your swing better than anybody," I said. "If you get into a rut, does he tell you what he sees?"

"Nah," Trout said, grinning, of course, because Trout always seems to be grinning. His joy is infectious. "He stopped coaching me when I was about 15."

Trout grew up in New Jersey, in the little town of Millville, and for Jeff and Debbie Trout, that means staying up very late on the East Coast to watch their son on the West Coast. "We text before and after every game," Trout said.

What does he text?

"He texts that he loves me, stuff like that."

Of course.

Later, I asked Jeff Trout about this, about the decisions that he and his wife had made in raising Mike and their two other children, Teal and Tyler. Jeff taught and coached at Millville High School, with great success, but as

Mike became a teenager and it was apparent that he was much faster than his peers and an elite athlete, Jeff decided to step back, to give Mike space. Roy Hallenbeck, Millville High's baseball coach, told me that Jeff didn't linger at practices, didn't inject himself into Mike's instruction, or lobby about his role. Jeff and Debbie went to games and cheered—for Mike, for his teammates. Jeff Trout held about every baseball record at Millville before Mike started to play, and Roy knew that Jeff had deep knowledge about the game.

But for the good of his son, for the sake of Mike's love of sports, Jeff Trout had backed away. By his senior year, Mike took down just about every one of his Dad's records, teasing him good-naturedly along the way. "There goes another one, Dad," Mike would joke.

He was a first-round pick of the Angels in 2009, and beyond his obvious speed and strength, what really jumped out at peers immediately was the joy with which Mike played. After Trout broke into the big leagues, Torii Hunter served as a mentor, and referred to Trout as a digger—when he ran to first base, the combination of his effort and size would cause him to create a rooster-tail of dirt flying up behind him.

Hunter would come to know Trouts' parents and years later, he would say that the choices they made along the way all paid off. Baseball's greatest player might also be one of its happiest, trading messages with family and friends before and after every game with words that have nothing to do with baseball and only about love and caring.

From that simple question to Trout outside of a batting cage, I learned a lesson that I've applied to my own family, a lesson for us all.

—*Buster Olney*, ESPN Senior Writer

01

BEGINNING

If the only reason I coached was to win basketball games,
my life would be pretty shallow.
-Mike Krzyzewski

Many of the most memorable moments in my life have occurred during sporting events. In nearly four decades as a member of the media I have seen the good, the bad, and the ugly. What transpires on the playing field can sometimes be far less memorable than what happens in the stands.

While most sports parents are supportive, others have exhibited behavior that has ruined the experience for those around them. Who are these individuals and what causes them to act so irrational?

I have witnessed outrageous displays ranging from parents coming out of the stands to join a huddle to others chewing out coaches who were doing postgame interviews.

The problem is only getting worse. On the same evening in the fall of 2018, I encountered two horrific examples of problems in sports, both likely involving parents. One featured an anonymous letter sent to a coach whose teams have competed in numerous state tournaments, but failed to win the championship. The letter called on the coach to have self-dignity and resign.

The other incident featured an argument in the stands between two individuals who happened to be cheering for the same team. The verbal attack turned personal and included a comment about a person's previous failed marriage. Just brutal. It made me sick to my stomach to watch that exchange.

Through the years I have witnessed all kinds of parents. While many are positive, there are others who think their son or daughter is the best player on the team and can do no wrong. I was determined not to fall into that trap. There was no way I was going to become one of "those parents."

I can honestly say, nothing prepared me for my own experience dealing with the parent trapped within.

Again, not all sport parents are bad. Most understand their roles. Unfortunately, some consider themselves experts on everything from coaching to officiating.

I've always told myself that I would never be like that, although in the back of my mind, I often wondered how I would react in similar situations. Would I be able to show some restraint or get sucked into the fray of raw emotions and ill-fated actions?

Being a member of the media (first as a sportswriter for the Aberdeen American News and now as a show host for Hub City Radio), I have trained myself to show a lack of emotion at nearly every event I have been at. Even when I have an opportunity to let loose, I simply am not a rah-rah person. Little did I know that my ability to stay calm and stoic would be put to the test like never before as my children took their turns filtering through the school system.

Throughout this book you will find a phrase that has resonated with me on my path as a parent of an athlete: sometimes parents view the game much differently than anyone else. As you will see, that can be both positive and negative.

While I don't have all the answers to solve the issue, I have witnessed enough bad behavior from parents to know that it is rampant. However, knowing about a problem and trying to avoid being a part of it can be two completely different things.

It is about 15 minutes before tip-off and I am in my usual spot behind the scorer's table prior to a postseason boys' basketball game at the Aberdeen Civic Arena.

I get a tap on my right shoulder and I turn around to find a middle-aged woman. She says, "Now, don't go putting what I say into the paper."

I am a bit puzzled at first, then realize she means she will not be responsible for whatever comes out of her mouth during the course of the next two hours. I explain to her that if she already realizes her temperament could be a problem, then she should understand she needs to be careful how she acts.

I tell her, "Listen, this is what it is. It's a ball game. This is not life and death."

I am not sure if my message sinks in, whether she is embarrassed by bringing it up in the first place, or maybe afraid that I actually will print what she shouts. Whatever the case, I don't have an issue with her the rest of the evening. I wish I could say that about all of my experiences.

I just can't understand why some fans feel the need to risk their life-long reputations over a ball game. Trust me, people may forgive, but they seldom forget.

My wife, Lauretta, and I are blessed to have two children. Mariah enjoys watching sports but did not participate in them much. Isaiah was involved in basketball and tennis. He played basketball for Aberdeen Christian and tennis for Aberdeen Roncalli through a cooperative arrangement because Christian did not offer tennis.

Interestingly enough, both Mariah and Isaiah got their first taste of organized basketball through Upward. It is a wonderful faith-based program that allows kids a chance to compete without all the pressures of main-stream society. Officials don't get berated, players aren't screamed at, and coaches aren't second guessed. In short, it's what you might expect elementary basketball to be.

While you might think that is the norm for players of that age group, trust me when I say that it isn't. I have been at multiple youth basketball and wrestling tournaments where youngsters end up in tears and officials are ready to eject spectators from facilities.

I somewhat understand the need to toughen up our children and not coddle them, but if players have a negative experience with a sport at the age of 9 or 10, they likely will not continue to play. And what does it tell them about our priorities as parents when all we care about is winning at all costs?

At that age, youngsters should not feel the weight of the world on their shoulders. They should not be allowed or worse yet, encouraged, to complain about questionable calls. They should not feel the need to live up to their parents' expectations.

In short, youth sports are the foundation for where everything starts, whether that's good habits, bad habits, unacceptable behavior or good sportsmanship.

That time period should also serve as a good proving ground for those same traits in parents. If they start yelling at the players, questioning the officials and second-guessing the coaches, chances are that behavior will continue if their sons or daughters continue playing into high school.

As a parent I have tried my best to remain positive and encouraging. Some nights are harder than others. My children will probably tell you that I've failed on many occasions.

While there will be many examples of Isaiah's games and matches in this book, rest assured I am equally proud of Mariah. We are all gifted with different talents and some of hers lie in the area of art. Her creative ability is off the charts. She can come home with an empty canvas, a set of paints and head downstairs. An hour later she emerges with a painting that could be sold at any craft fair. I really have no idea how she can do that.

I think that having a background in a certain area probably leads to a greater appreciation for what our children are going through. Unfortunately, it can also lead us to have more demanding expectations. For instance, I was never much of a basketball player, so when our kids played, I was probably more of a fan than a critic (although Lauretta might argue otherwise).

While I was never a standout tennis player, my wife and I still play and have been in many competitive matches. Justified or not, it probably gives me more of a sense of authority when it comes to providing advice in that sport. Additionally, it also provides more of an appreciation of certain things on the court because I have been in those situations.

It is a summer evening and Isaiah and I are playing a men's league doubles match. It will mark the only summer that Isaiah and I are partners, because he will soon be much better than me and will want a different partner.

We are receiving serve and one of the opponents on this night is a hard-serving lefthander. He doesn't get a high percentage of serves in, but when he does, they are very difficult to return.

The guy serves a bullet right up the T to Isaiah's backhand. It is clearly a ball with plenty of juice on it and Isaiah takes a full swing at it. He is behind the pace and pushes the ball wide.

I look over and think to myself, "Why on earth did you take a full swing at that ball?"

It is a serve that I would have blocked back, used the other's guy pace, and kept the ball in play.

Four games later, the same exact thing happens. The server pounds a serve up the middle to Isaiah's backhand. Isaiah again takes a full swing at the ball. Only this time he crushes a return winner on a ball hit so hard it looks like it has a vapor trail behind it. The opponents don't even have time to flinch as the return winner blazes past them.

I look over and think to myself, "I guess I understand why you took a full swing at that ball."

And then came the sudden realization: man, I wish just once in my life I could hit a return of serve off my backhand like that.

We can teach our children all kinds of drills and provide all kinds of advice. But until we are actually in their exact situation, we may never know how we ourselves would react to their circumstances. It is lesson that would serve us all well.

02

VANTAGE POINT

*Little things make the difference. Everyone is well prepared in
the big things, but only the winners perfect the little things.*
—*Paul Bear Bryant*

When people think of sports, the first thing that comes to mind is physical presence; it's what people can see; it's what others can readily measure. How fast can you run, how high can you jump, how much do you weigh, how much can you lift, and how tall are you in bare feet?

What is far more compelling to me is the mental side of sports. It's the intangible that you can't readily define, is difficult to measure, but is very obvious when on display.

I once did an entire project on the psychology of sports. It was fascinating to get inside the mind of coaches and athletes to see what motivated them and what often proved to be the difference between success and failure. I've interviewed thousands of athletes through the years. I cannot recall a single one that ever rated the mental part of their particular sport at less than 50 percent and most put it as high as 80 or 90 percent.

I guess that it only stands to reason that coaches try their best to say the right things to get their athletes to reach their full potential. Some do it before games. Others will save their best material for halftimes. If needed, some will even do it while an event is in progress.

It's championship night of a state basketball tournament. As the two teams prepare for the announcement of the starting lineups, the coach of the underdog squad on this occasion has a few last-minute words of advice for his players.

He looks his athletes in the eye and says with conviction, "Best team wins. Not best player. Not best players. Best team wins."

It is the right speech, because I know that his squad will be up against it in a matter of a few short minutes. Those choice words will likely get his players to believe that they can pull off the upset.

While the methodology and philosophy are well thought out and practical, there is no substitute for talent. His team loses soundly to a powerhouse. The coach is absolutely correct when he says, "best team wins." It's just that on this particular occasion, the other team is better than his.

Personally, I think that the power of positive reinforcement is much better than criticism. Most people need a boost more than we realize. In fact, studies have shown individuals will work much harder if they know what they do is appreciated.

I know of some coaches who were particularly hard on their players but made sure that positive comments outweighed the negative and always tried to end the conservation on a good note.

I really enjoy the wisdom of the late legendary UCLA basketball coach John Wooden. One of the things that he said is, "Praise is a great motivator. Criticism is a great teaching tool if done properly, but praise is the best motivator."

What I find really interesting is what parents will say to their children to try to motivate and encourage them. Again, I would much rather see building up than tearing down, however sometimes even the most well-intentioned comments do not help much because those not participating in the contests can have a much different perspective than those who are.

It's getting late in the race during the state cross-country meet in Huron. Runners are beginning to hit the wall as they approach the final incline out on the course.

A father spots his daughter coming up the way. He positions himself to make sure that his daughter can see him as she begins her ascent up the hill.

She appears to be struggling as she approaches. As she runs by, the dad yells, "You're not tired! You're not tired!"

The girl glances over at her father and shoots him a stare that could have killed anybody in that exact moment. She continues to lumber past us on the way to the finish line, still a long way off in the distance.

As the girl moves on, the dad looks over at me and says knowingly, "She's tired."

I smile and think to myself, well so much for that bit of psychology.

(Sometimes parents view things much differently than anyone else.)

As a parent, I've found myself saying things like, "keep working; hang in there; you're all right."

You never know when an encouraging word might make a difference. It sure beats the alternative.

However, I also have been around the game long enough to know when an athlete is on the ropes. Body language always conveys much more than verbal language when it comes to a person's mindset. It doesn't matter the sport, it doesn't matter the significance of the contest: when the shoulders slump and the head bows, it's generally over.

Conversely, I've seen body language come to life during a contest. The most dangerous foe is one that genuinely believes it can win. I've seen many underdogs who hang around and hang around and there comes a time when it sinks in that they really can pull off the upset. It's a beautiful thing to see in young people, who suddenly understand that they have what it takes to compete and be successful.

Of course, I've seen just the opposite on more than one occasion when a team is beat the second it leaves the bus, because it has no confidence whatsoever that it can be victorious.

Again, it all starts with the coach and works its way down to the players. If a coach does not believe in a team's ability to win, chances are that team won't win. Now, it's not as basic as wanting to be successful or even believing that you will be.

Sometimes coaches and parents confuse determination for mental toughness.

A while back, I heard a coach talk before a big playoff game and he said the outcome would all come down to who wanted it more. I know this is a popular phrase in today's sports realm, but I don't believe it's a wise one.

For starters, I have never met an athlete who did not want to win. Nobody likes to lose. By telling athletes it comes down to who wants it more, you are setting them up for failure. There are far more important elements in games than sheer desire, like strategy, execution and talent.

So, let's say that your team loses (as was the case with the aforementioned coach). Now, you have your players that are feeling responsible for losing the game because they weren't determined enough. Never mind the fact that the opposing team might have had far superior players and you might not have beaten them had you played them 10 times. Secondly, you are now discrediting the other team, saying you didn't really beat us, we just didn't want it bad enough. That makes absolutely no sense.

I totally understand the power of determination. Sometimes it can prove to be the difference when more talented athletes are disinterested. We've all heard the saying, hard work beats talent when talent doesn't work hard. However, when talented individuals are highly motivated, that's a tough combination to overcome and sheer willpower likely won't be enough to do it.

One of the reasons I love track and field is because that determination and competitive spirit is often on display. While others watch the leaders in particular races, I often keep an eye on the others back in the pack. I like to see what individuals have inside of them when they know they have no chance of winning but are confronted with a challenge of trying to catch or hold off another runner.

Some wilt under the pressure, others dig deep, find another gear and meet that challenge. To me, those are the truly successful athletes, the ones who find a way to maximize their full potential and compete like it's their last race ever, even though winning is not in the realm of possibility.

Of course, when you are truly gifted, it's always a bit easier to meet that challenge, no matter how unrealistic conditions might seem.

It's the Class B boys' 1,600-meter relay at the 2005 state track and field meet at Howard Wood Stadium in Sioux Falls. The event is the final one of the state meet each year to cap off the season. It's a race that all coaches like to stack and save their best runners for which makes it even more compelling.

The final leg of the mile relay often features the best of the best 400-meter runners in the state. On this particular year, the top quarter-miler for Class B boys is Dan Young of Northwestern High School. Like always, I am perched near the finish line as the race is in progress.

The Northwestern squad appears to be in big trouble. The Wildcats are way behind on the third leg of the race. They have Young anchoring the final leg, but he will have his work cut out for him. As the runners come in approaching the final hand off, Northwestern is in a distant third place.

I glance over at Young who is sizing up the amount of ground he will have to make up once he gets the baton for the final leg. He looks at the distance between first place and his teammate who is in third place. He then smiles and nods his head. I know the race is over.

I can hardly wait for what will transpire, because I know that the state's premier 400-meter runner believes he can pull this off and he has the talent to do it. As Young embarks on a memorable sprint around the track I marvel at what I am witnessing. This is what happens when supreme talent intersects with divine confidence.

Young wins the race going away, making some of the state's other top sprinters look slow in the process.

Of course, confidence in your ability doesn't have to mean that you're necessarily the best athlete. It might mean that you have a very good skill set. The bottom line is, if you're good at what you do and you believe that you can do it as well or better than anybody else, you are a dangerous foe.

Now, that belief does not come by accident. It comes by doing. You have to have experiences that you can draw upon to make that confidence or mental toughness relevant. Otherwise, we're back to who wants it more and most times determination by itself is never enough.

While auto racing is a sport, most racers are probably not considered athletic by nature. However, the same principles apply when it comes to preparation, mental toughness and talent. One of the best drivers I have ever covered is Kent Arment from Aberdeen. He finds a way to combine those elements into his racing style.

It's a Friday night at Brown County Speedway and the Modified feature is nearing an end. Kent Arment has given it a good run, but it appears that he is destined for second place on this particular evening.

I begin to head to the scales in the middle of the infield so I can interview the winning driver, before he heads to the pits. As I walk across the infield on the final lap, I notice that Arment is not backing off coming out of turn number two.

Now, I know that Arment is a competitor at heart, but I think there is no way that he is going to be able to win this race. In fact, most drivers, no matter how

*talented, would have just settled for second and moved on. I stop walking to watch
the rest of the race unfold as Arment somehow manages to catch the leader on the
final turn and race past him just in time to take the checkered flag.*

*I shake my head at what I just witness. As Arment pulls up to the scale, I ask
him, "Did you think you were going to win that race?"*

Arment responds matter-of-factly, "I think I'm going to win every race."

That self-confidence and mental toughness, combined with supreme
ability, is what separates the elite from the others.

Can you coach mental toughness? Can parents bring that out in their
children?

I do believe athletes can be motivated to do their best. However, true
determination and drive has to come from within. A coach or a parent can
never want it worse than the athlete. It never works, because that means that
either the parent is too invested in the situation or the athlete is not invested
enough. Either way, that's not a good formula for success.

03

OFFICIALLY SPEAKING

Don't whine, don't complain, don't make excuses.
Just do the best you can.
—John Wooden

Second-guessing the calls of officials, referees and umpires has been around as long as the games themselves. Some might argue that it is a part of the very fabric of our sporting world.

While that may be, it doesn't mean that it's always warranted and it certainly doesn't mean that it's the right thing to do.

And trust me, it starts long before the games should have any sort of major consequence. Longtime friend and volunteer official Don Peck of Aberdeen witnessed his share of poor parental behavior while working games at the local YMCA Tournament for nearly 20 years.

"I was experienced and in my younger days did the older kids games. Later I asked to do smaller gyms (easier on my joints) and was tasked with officiating fourth grade," Peck said. "While it was easier on me physically, it was far more challenging on the spirit. While it was not the majority of the games, it was almost a guarantee that there would be a parent or two (or three…) that would be an embarrassment to what the Y was trying to accomplish."

In fact, the abuse got so bad that Don once offered to change places with a parent.

"On one occasion the father was so abusive of the refereeing, that I stopped the game and offered him my whistle to complete the game," Peck recalled. "While he glared at me in disgust, it did silence him."

Keep in mind these were fourth-grade games.

Don said the majority of the issues started with the parents and then eventually carried over to those involved in the game.

"I also remember during a break of play, that I advised the coach of one team that if he did not control the crowd (parents), I was going to assert a technical foul," Peck said. "The sad element is that at the start of the game the kids were enthusiastic and focused on competing. But more than once, I noticed that the unhealthy frenzy coming from the parents impacted the play on the court. Rather than continuing to have fun and enjoy the game, the kids were more inclined to be disrespectful, not only to each other, but to the officiating as well."

Currently there is a shortage of officials in South Dakota and it is no wonder why. Officials are often the scape goat for everything. From media to fans to coaches to players, officials often are questioned, criticized and blamed for the final outcome of contests.

Let's be very clear. As long as there is a human element to the game, there are always going to be mistakes made. That goes for the players and coaches as well as the officials. I have been covering sports for nearly 40 years and I can honestly say that I have never witnessed one act of blatant favoritism on the part of an official. Questionable calls? Yes. The wrong calls? Perhaps. An obvious intent to favor one team over another? Never.

I totally understand a coach's desire to get every call in a contest. And trust me, it doesn't have to be in the final minute of overtime for that desire to take place.

It's a cold night in February, but the mood inside the packed gym is hot. The contest which is about to begin features two of the top basketball teams in the state. While it is still the regular season, there is plenty at stake, like a conference championship and post-season seed points.

As the players head to the sidelines to get ready for the introduction of the starting lineups, the announcer reads a statement that is heard before most high school contests. It comes directly from the South Dakota High School Activities Association. It is a creed about sportsmanship and includes a line about respecting the judgment of the officials.

It is less than five minutes later that the opening tip takes place and within seven seconds an official makes a call that does not get full approval. The coach whose team did not benefit from the call wastes no time at all complaining to the ref that he missed it. I guess that opening statement was just a waste of breath for that announcer, because before the night is over, more than one person takes exception with the calls of the officials on the floor.

While coaches might think they are justified in fighting for their players, they can and do cross the line on occasion. It has been my experience that some coaches, especially those with lengthy years of service or outstanding records, get a little longer leash than others. (Notice I did not say, get a few more calls than others). I know that in the heat of the moment, some of those coaches, well intentioned or not, have said things that they later regretted.

Former Aberdeen Roncalli High School football coach Terry Dosch once told me that he went too far one night. During one of his games, he berated an official so bad, that the next morning he called that individual up to apologize. It turned out that the referee, a longtime friend, had been a member of Dosch's wedding party.

"I've made some painful mistakes," Dosch said when recalling the moment. "Afterwards, I was thinking, 'Man, c'mon, what are you doing? There is nothing that I want more than to show my players than you can compete and be a good Christian person at the same time." (American News Feb. 19, 1999)

I've seen players talk back to officials. It goes without saying that should never happen. So where do the players get off thinking it's appropriate to question the calls of officials?

More times than not it comes straight from mom and dad. I have heard more complaining coming from the stands than anywhere else during games. And I can honestly say, that in many cases, the individual who often screams the loudest is the most uneducated when it comes to the rules of the game.

Of course, there are people who understand the game inside and out who still complain. On more than one occasion I have witnessed a parent who is a certified official, criticize a working official during a game in which his son or daughter is playing.

I recently asked a respected official who had a child competing in sports if he ever yelled at a ref during a game. I respect his honesty when he paused and somewhat sheepishly held up his hand indicating it has happened about four or five times.

He went on to explain that it's hard not to get emotional when the contest involves a family member. He then cited an example of another parent who is an official who hollers far more than he does.

(Sounds to me like the parent trapped within).

I have always told myself that officials are human and they do the best they can to get every call right. I have never been one to blame the refs for the outcome of a game. However, when your son is on the floor, it's easy to get sucked into the moment.

It's a tight contest in Langford. Aberdeen Christian is battling the Lions on even terms in the first half. The contest is intense and the fans are into it.

The officials are some of the best in the state and I know them on a personal basis. There will be no hint of favoritism throughout the game.

Yet, there is a call that goes against one of my son's teammates. As the fans around start to stir, I shout, "That wasn't traveling the other night in Britton!"

While that may seem tame compared to what many fans in gyms across the country yell at officials, it clearly crosses the line for me. I think to myself, oh no, am I becoming one of "those parents?"

(Sometimes parents view things much differently than anyone else.)

I have never been one to buy into the notion that a call cost some team a game. To me, that just gives those involved in the contest a reason to believe that they did not control their own destiny.

In my opinion, good teams make plays, average teams make excuses.

I have been at games where fans will take one look at the officials long before the game begins and say, "Well, we've got no chance tonight." Really?

So where do fans figure that they have the right to complain and yell at every call that does not go their way?

Well, for starters, some think that if they pay the price of admission that it gives them the power to be heard. Others simply have too much pride to accept that, regardless of what calls are made, the other team might just be better on that given night.

However, I think part of the problem stems from the media. Talk radio has gotten out of control with well-known announcers blaming officials for calls that they think have swayed certain contests. Unfortunately, it is even becoming more commonplace with play-by-play announcers.

Since when did it become the media's job to critique officials? I have been a working member of the media for 38 years and I never once noticed that in my job description.

When the media becomes biased and starts to second guess officials (and trust me it's gotten much worse in recent years through the advent of social media), it seems only natural that it will embolden and empower those who sit in the stands.

It has been my experience that officials are trained, educated and more times than not get the calls correct. Even in this day and age of technology reviewing plays from every angle possible, slowing down the action to still images, it amazes me how officials in real time are able to get the calls right.

Like I feel about coaches, many of my friends are officials. Pick the sport: baseball, wrestling, football, volleyball, I personally know officials in all of them. I respect them for the job that they do. Are they perfect? Not hardly. But I admire and appreciate their willingness to help officiate games that provide life-long lessons for those who play them.

04

LEADERSHIP

Leadership is a matter of having people look at you and gain confidence seeing how you react. If you're in control, they're in control.
—*Tom Landry*

If there is one common trait of all the successful teams that I have covered through the years it is solid leadership and it starts from the top down. Most winning programs have stability in the coaching ranks.

While there have been very rare occasions where teams have exceled despite inexperienced coaches, for the most part, you show me a successful team and I'll show you a knowledgeable coach who instructs, inspires and motivates.

The best coaches not only have a passion for what they do, they put players in a position to succeed and most importantly they get individuals to believe in themselves and in the system.

It is a weekday afternoon in Watertown. Aberdeen Roncalli is playing tennis against the host Arrows and Isaiah has his hands full against a solid Watertown player. During one of the changeovers in between games, Isaiah comes over to the fence and talks to his coach JD Carrels.

The conversation goes something like this: "Coach, when I get my serve in, he can't get it back," Isaiah says. To which Coach Carrels responds, "When you serve like that, nobody's getting it back."

I can't even imagine how that would make me feel as a player. If that doesn't give you confidence, nothing will.

I recently talked to a coach who said it really doesn't matter how good a scheme is, if the players buy into the system and have faith that it will work, it will. Conversely, the opposite is also true. No matter how good the playbook or strategy, if players do not have the confidence to execute it, it probably won't work.

Talent is never enough. I have covered many talented players and teams that never reached their full potential because they were never on the same page. When the huddles in the timeout turn into a shouting match, chaos is right around the corner.

To carry this a step further, when the players start arguing with the officials and with each other, it seldom works out well. But again, it all starts at the top. I've always said, you show me a team that's out of control and I'll show you a coach that's out of control.

One of the guests on my Legends Sports Show (a weekly program featuring stars of the past), multiple hall of fame member Bob Swanhorst, told me the one common trait of every good squad is players who are willing to sacrifice for the good of the team and get along with each other.

"Without a doubt, there is absolutely no question in my mind talent is always subordinate to kids getting along. If you don't have cooperation with teammates you'll never go anyplace. And I see that over and over and over again with the team players. If that doesn't happen it's not going to work. I think if you see a really good basketball team, I will almost ensure that all five of them get along very well." (The Legends Sports Show, Feb. 22, 2018)

Now, I understand there are times when not everybody will agree on everything, but when you hit the playing surface, there simply cannot be a battle of egos on the line.

Again, it all starts with leadership at the top. This is true in every walk of life, whether it is in the business world or the athletic arena. Somebody has to set the tone and that needs to be the leader. When times are difficult, if the leader demonstrates confidence and self-control, the employees or players will be more apt to produce under pressure. If the leader reaches for the panic button, chances are the others will follow suit and it will be a no-win situation.

Most veteran coaches understand the concept of setting the tone for their squads. Very few teams are going to win every time out, but if you prepare to win each game, your chances at victory are much greater.

I once interviewed a coach at the start of a football season and asked what was realistic for his squad for the upcoming season. He looked at me and stated that he expected to win every game. He said he wasn't going to concede any of them as losses.

Now he and I both knew that running the table would be difficult, but I also understood the message he was sending to his players. He wasn't going to say they would be .500 or even 6-2, because that would imply that he didn't think his team was capable of defeating several opponents on the schedule.

Players come and go, but coaches who are battle tested and instill confidence in their players always seem to have solid squads. There was an individual not long ago whose team continued to win one close game after another. As I talked about that fact with a knowledgeable basketball person, he said, "You know what that is? That's coaching."

While X's and O's are valuable, it's more than that. It's understanding how to shape and mold the individuals that are on your team, getting them to buy into the team concept and understand that no one person is bigger than the squad.

Does that mean that all members of the team are equal in talent and ability? Not hardly. But what it does mean is that when leadership, whether exhibited by a business owner or by a coach, has a game plan that is effective and if others understand their roles and do their jobs, success will follow. If you don't believe me, just take a look at the New England Patriots or Connecticut women's basketball team.

One of the most successful teams I ever covered, the Sisseton High School girls' basketball squad of the early 2000s, was a perfect example of a "team." The team had a scorer, a ballhandler, a rebounder, a lock-down defender, someone to do the tough jobs, like setting screens to get teammates open. In short, everybody had a job to do, the coaches placed them in the best possible position to perform those tasks and that team was very difficult to beat. Sisseton won three Class A state championships in four years during that run and was runner-up the other year.

Does everybody want to be the star player, make the last-second shot, be the one that gets all the attention? It's only human nature to want those things (even if some people can't really handle the pressure). However, if each member of the team tried to accomplish that, they would all fall short of reaching their potential, both individually and as a team. The best teams are not the ones with the most talented players. They're the ones that play the best together and again that all starts with leadership set by the coach.

Of course, it never hurts when those leadership traits are exhibited by the players. That's why captains and seniors are so valuable for setting the tone. There was one coach I used to cover who said each season, "We'll go as far as our seniors take us."

As the Saturday boys' basketball game in Ipswich comes to a close, the mood is fairly upbeat. Aberdeen Christian overcomes a slow start to beat a solid Ipswich squad. However, it is not a great offensive game for Isaiah.

Just when I am feeling frustrated, Knights coach David Rohrbach points out some of the things that Isaiah does to help the team, like playing solid defense and handling the basketball. "That's the thing I like about him. You always get the same player. He doesn't let a bad shooting game affect the other parts of his game," Coach Rohrbach says.

(Sometimes parents view things much differently than anyone else.)

It's definitely possible to win significant games with a majority of underclassmen, but most of the successful squads that I can recall had solid leadership, first from the coach and then with at least one or two seniors who often brought more to the table than just points or touchdowns. There is no substitute for experience and maturity.

There have been rare occasions where teams have won championships without any seniors. However, when that happens, somebody still has to set the tone. It goes without saying that it all starts with the coach and then a player or two has to step up and perform beyond their years. And chances are, those underclassmen likely emulated behavior traits they picked up from an older player in practice the year before.

If there is one thing I have found to be true in nearly every sport through the years is that if talent and coaching between the two squads is somewhat even, the team that has a group of motivated seniors will prevail most of the time.

05

PERSPECTIVE

A good coach can change a game.
A great coach can change a life.
—*John Wooden*

Coaches are an interesting group of people. They come in all shapes and sizes, and possess multiple ranges of intensity and moods. Many of my best friends are current coaches or former coaches.

While I have a great deal of respect for most coaches, I do think some of them are a bit misguided. When the focus of the contest is on the coaches and their antics instead of the action on the field or on the floor, the coaches have lost their perspective on the games. The contests are for the players, more than the coaches or the fans.

I totally understand the need for leadership and control. Most coaches dictate all schemes, from stunts on defense in football to sideline plays in basketball. And they should, because they have the experience and they know their personnel better than anyone. I would be disappointed in any coach who just sits and watches the game and has little to no impact on it at all.

However, sometimes coaches can carry things a bit too far. I know of several coaches who have told me, they hate losing more than they enjoy winning. That leads me to believe that their stake in the game is likely much higher than anybody else's. And if there is one thing I have learned in covering athletics through the years, it's that neither the parents nor the coaches should want it worse than the athletes. It simply cannot not work that way. If the players fail to match the intensity of the coach, it indicates one of two things: a group of players who aren't all in, or a coach that is way too invested. Either way, it can be a precursor to rough times ahead.

There's a fine line between passion and obsession. Players feed off the positive energy of a coach. They can wilt when the coach becomes so demanding that the game is no longer fun and they feel like they can do nothing right. There is nothing wrong with hard coaching. There is plenty wrong when it comes to verbal and physical abuse.

I once heard a coach describe one of his players as "absolutely worthless," in front of the rest of the team. It is during times like those when you begin to wonder if the outcome of the game has become too important. Many teenagers have so much going on in their lives as it is. The last thing they need is to be belittled in front of their peers.

It is a relatively normal night as I cover a girls' basketball game. The contest will likely blend in among the countless other games I have witnessed until a bizarre scene unfolds in front of hundreds of spectators.

One of the players is having a rough night and her coach has had enough. He calls timeout and the players head over to the bench. However, the coach meets this particular player nearly halfway out on the floor and begins to yell at her. As she walks away to go join her teammates, the coach grabs her arm and forcefully stops her.

It is not a good scene and it is about to get much, much worse. As the player joins her teammates on the bench and the coach comes over, the girls' dad gets up from his bleacher seat. He proceeds to walk straight across the floor and over to the huddle. The gym grows eerily silent.

The dad taps the coach on the shoulder and says, "I don't want you touching my daughter."

A brief discussion takes place, and the game resumes, but the damage is already done on multiple levels. The coach, I'm sure is embarrassed, the parent will likely always be remembered for that, and the poor girl in the spotlight cannot find a hole big enough to crawl into.

(Another example of the parent trapped within.)

I am not going to tell you for one minute that the parent did not have a right to complain about the way the coach treated his daughter, but there is a time and place for everything. The discussion that ensued needed to take place after the game when cooler heads prevailed and the audience did not have a front-row seat to the altercation.

Look, I know that nobody likes to lose. Some people are way more competitive than others. But as a coach, you're representing your school and you have to set the tone for your players. If intensity is required that's fine, but if self-restraint is needed, then it should take place.

I know that coaches are a bundle of energy, especially on game day. I've watched normal, rational people who I consider to be close friends turn into almost total strangers before, during and immediately following contests. I've had some take out their losses on me. I've had some blame the officials. There are some that looked so angry I was almost afraid to ask a question during a post-game interview.

His team had not played well, at least from what I was anticipating. His squad had lost and while some reporters don't normally interview losing coaches, I always like to give coaches from both teams an opportunity for comment, win or lose.

As he exits the locker room, we stand next to each other without anybody around. I ask him a simple question and he explodes. He goes into a 30-second profanity laced tirade, blaming anything and anyone he can think of, mainly the officials. If he was a total stranger, I might just turn my back and leave.

He is not. He happens to be an intelligent man who knows the game inside and out and a longtime friend. Clearly, I have not given him enough time to blow off steam before I get to him.

Following his R-rated synopsis of the game, I calmly look over and say, "Really? Because from where I was sitting it looked like your guys' shoes were nailed to the floor and you had no energy at all tonight."

That takes some guts, but it has to be said.

He looks over at me and realizing I am not buying what he is selling, pauses and says, "I don't know what our problem was. We just couldn't do anything."

Had the game become much more meaningful to him than it should have?

As a member of the media, I understand there is a fine line between rushing in for an interview to catch the raw emotion of a last-second victory, and not giving someone enough time to cool off after a frustrating defeat. It is a lesson that I have learned through the years, sometimes the hard way. And I always make sure that I don't hang somebody out to dry because in the heat of the moment they say something they could regret for a lifetime.

So, what could possess a coach to act so out of character on game day? Well, part of it is because coaches feel responsible for their team's success. They also feel like their reputations are on the line. And in some respects, they are.

Look, for the most part coaches are in a no-win situation. When they win, often the margin is not big enough to impress the parents or the boosters. If they lose, the blame often falls squarely on their shoulders. Coaches are the easiest scapegoats when things go wrong.

There is a lot of truth that the best place to coach is in an orphanage.

I once had a head basketball coach tell me that one year his team lost just two games but fell just short in its quest of getting to the state tournament. Before he could exit the gym that evening, a school board member came up to him and said, "You better get your resume in order because you're not coaching here next year." And he didn't.

I know of another highly successful coach who year after year had one of the top teams in the state. He told me of several anonymous letters he received in the mail telling him what a disgrace he was and that he needed to walk away from coaching.

There was another individual who coached a team that was undefeated all the way up to the state championship game. His team lost in that title contest. Following an argument with administration over his coaching abilities, he did not return the following season.

Is it any wonder why coaches feel pressure to win and why maybe ball games become more than just ball games?

Some of my best friends have gotten out of coaching, not because of the athletes, but because of the parents and the administration. Others remain in coaching and talk about getting out just because of the stress surrounding their profession.

These individuals help to shape and mold our youth and get pennies on the dollar for doing it. They are more influential than most adults our kids will encounter in their lifetimes. And most do it because they love teaching teenagers and watching them grow into mature adults.

I talked to a man not long ago who was a highly successful wrestling coach. He told me one of the greatest satisfactions in his career was knowing that he had likely helped to keep some guys out of jail and get them back on the right path because of the sport. To me, that means more than any wins or losses on a coach's resume.

Sometimes coaches impact far more people than just those on their team.

One of the most memorable moments that I witnessed in recent years involved a coach but had nothing to do with the final outcome of the contest.

Prior to the Aberdeen Christian-Summit boys' basketball game Jessica Rohrbach was preparing to sing the National Anthem. Jessica, who was 12 at the time, has Williams Syndrome and was filling in for her ill sister that evening.

Jessica had performed the anthem at Special Olympics events, a college basketball game and other events. However, on this night, there was no CD player available so she decided to try to sing the anthem a cappella for the first time.

Unfortunately, she started the song too high and soon found herself in trouble. That's when then Summit players decided to join in and soon everybody was singing the anthem. Feeling the support she needed, Jessica jumped right back in and led the crowd the rest of the way in a rousing rendition of the song.

"Once the young lady kind of struggled, I started to sing," said then Summit coach Derrick Rauen. "A couple of my seniors followed along. Before I knew it, the whole team was chiming in."

The coach said he wouldn't have wanted to trade places with Rohrbach but was inspired that she was able to regain her composure and lead everybody in the rest of the song.

"I thought that was the nicest moment of the entire anthem is when she did come along and take the lead and take us home with it." (American News, January 8, 2015).

The best coaches instruct and inspire, shape and strengthen, mold and motivate. If they happen to win a bunch of games along the way, so much the better.

06

INTEGRITY

*I hate to lose worse than anything, but if you never lose you won't
know how to act. If you lose with humility, then you can come back.*
—*Paul Bear Bryant*

Let's operate under the assumption that everybody wants to win no matter
what sport they play. Some understand that others are far more gifted and
talented meaning that winning a particular contest is next to impossible,
but that doesn't mean they like to lose or don't care about the outcome.

For the most part, nearly every athlete appears to be relatively happy
when things are going well and wins are mounting up. However, I have
always believed you can tell a person's true character and integrity when
things are not going well. I have witnessed tennis players who have thrown
their racquets, thrown their bags, kicked their bags and even one player who
broke his racquet by smashing it against his foot in disgust during a match.

I pay pretty close attention regarding how an athlete or a coach reacts
when a loss occurs, especially when it is not expected.

*It's a Saturday night in late January and Golden Eagles Arena is full of avid
wrestling fans. It's the Annual Lee Wolf Invitational, bringing together some of
the top wrestlers in a two-state area.*

I am armed with a notebook, a micro-cassette recorder and a little flip recorder to shoot video. I plot out my strategy, figuring out which area athletes are in the finals and which matches I will need to cover.

As the night moves on, I shoot video, interview athletes and lay the foundation for the next day's story.

I have no idea that the night will turn into something neither I nor the hundreds in attendance will ever forget.

A wrestler from the coverage area finishes off an opponent and like I have done with other athletes, I follow him off the mat to grab a quick interview before turning my attention to the next match.

It just so happens that this particular wrestler is having a conversation with his coach that lasts a bit longer than normal. I know I need to get moving, because the country's top wrestler Logan Storley of Webster is up next. By the time I finish the interview and head back to the mat, Storley is rolling as usual.

The winner of 196 consecutive matches is up on Preston Lehmann of West Fargo, North Dakota 15-2 after two periods. Storley is just two points away from a technical fall and I realize I have not shot one second of video of his match. I figure, I will just shoot whatever I can before he scores two mores points and gets his hand raised. It won't be ideal, but it's the best I can do for now.

As I focus my flip recorder on the mat, the unthinkable happens. Storley, who has lost just two matches in his entire six-year high school career, gets caught in a move and is on his back. The crowd begins to buzz as they realize what is taking place. How in the world can this be happening?

Storley, who has dominated this match, is now in major trouble and a few seconds later is pinned for the only time in his illustrious high school career. I cannot believe what I am videotaping.

When the match ends, I glance into the crowd. People are on their phones alerting those not in attendance to what they have just witnessed. There is a buzz in the building that lasts the rest of the evening. Under normal circumstances I would not have even shot the sequence. I would have taken enough video of Storley on his way to the commanding lead, that I would have stopped long before then.

Instead, I have a video that will be viewed by hundreds before the night is over.

Now comes the difficult part. I have a huge story on my hands, but I wonder how Storley will handle this unforeseeable circumstance. Will he talk to me? I won't blame him if he doesn't, but this is THE story. This is what others will be talking about more than any other match of the tourney.

I approach him a short while after the match and ask if he is willing to share a few thoughts. I tell him he certainly doesn't have to, but that this is what people will be discussing and I am going to report on it.

To his credit, Logan agrees to an interview. While he is obviously disappointed, stunned and I am sure very angry, he is very forthcoming.

"I didn't think it was going to happen," Storley says. "I got lazy. He's a tough kid and he caught me and stuck me. I can't do anything about it but regroup and come back for districts, regions and state. At least it was now and not the state tournament." (American News, Jan. 30, 2011)

There he was, the teen who is used to being in the spotlight for all his major accomplishments, now the center of attention for something he certainly doesn't want and for sure isn't expecting. He manages the situation as well or better than one can expect a high school student under a microscope to do. I walk away from our conversation knowing that Storley will be just fine in his quest for a sixth consecutive state championship.

About a month later, Storley won that sixth straight state title. And I know that his loss at the Lee Wolf probably played a motivating role to make sure he would finish his high school career the same way he started it: at the top.

Storley was later named the Hodge Award winner, given to the top high school wrestler in the nation regardless of state or weight class. Lehmann went on to wrestle at the University of Nebraska, while Storley went on to have an outstanding career at the University of Minnesota and is now competing in MMA.

Now that I think about it, it makes me think about a lesson that I learned from Lee Wolf himself. He happened to be my gym teacher in junior high. I will always recall something that he told our class many, many years ago.

He said, "Just remember, no matter what you do in life, there will always be somebody better than you and always somebody worse than you."

There is a lot of truth in that statement. And if you take those words to the extreme and you do pit the best against the best, the same individual or team does not always win every time.

As a parent, you always want your child to experience success and to be a part of the winning team. Needless to say, that doesn't always happen.

However, society has a bit of a warped idea of what success really means. The world's definition of success is who wins the championship, who scores the most points, who wins the most times.

Now, I am not a huge fan of today's philosophy of everybody gets a trophy or a medal. In fact, I think sometimes we try appease all those who play and try not to hurt anybody's feelings. But to me, there is much, much more involved in athletics than just those who win or lose.

I believe that success can best be defined by giving a God-honoring effort. If you do that, regardless of the outcome, you are a success.

It is the day after a season-ending loss in the boys' basketball district tournament. Aberdeen Christian had lost in an intense contest that featured plenty of raw emotion.

I am out at the school running an errand when a staff member approaches me. She says that she was very proud of Isaiah during the game. My initial thought was why? He hadn't played particularly well and really had very little impact on the contest. Or so I thought.

She explains that she had watched his actions and that when things started getting a little rough, Isaiah calmed down his teammates and helped to keep their emotions in check.

I am impressed she noticed that and a bit embarrassed I had not. I thank her for the comments and point out that is part of being a team captain. That he should know that being a captain is more than just having a title. That it meant responsibility for setting the tone for the team. Still, I walk away with a good feeling knowing he had indeed made an impact in that contest, even though I had completely missed it.

(Sometimes parents view things differently than anyone else.)

I have witnessed good, bad and indifferent behavior at the result of athletic events. Trust me, I have seen plenty of meltdowns, plenty of tears and plenty of finger-pointing. I have seen athletes and coaches chase officials off the floor. I have seen parents lambast coaches. It can be a surreal environment.

While most of the lack of sportsmanship can be traced back to teams or individuals who have lost, it is not exclusive to that side of the ledger. In fact, I will say this as clear as I possibly can: the only thing worse than a poor loser is a poor winner.

This point was driven home a long time ago while I was at an American Legion baseball tournament. As is the case with many baseball games, there was a lot of chatter and banter that went on throughout the game. However, as one side began to pull away from the other, the team destined to win became even louder and more obnoxious.

At the end of that game, there was not a good spirit on that field.

I totally understand the desire to win and the instruction to play hard until the final whistle. Players should never be instructed to give less than their best in any situation. However, there is a right way and wrong way to play and conduct yourself.

Taunting is never acceptable and running up the score or rubbing it in falls under the same category.

I can't tell you how many times tempers have flared and blood has boiled because of the desire to get one more basket, one more touchdown or beat a team beyond submission.

I have witnessed teams pressing other teams despite being up by more than 50 points. I have seen coaches leave their starters in to pad their stats. I recall one night of an intense game that was finally decided in the closing seconds. As the winning team was running out the clock, its coach instructed a player to pass the ball ahead to get one more basket before the final buzzer instead of dribbling out the remaining time on the clock. There was no handshake between the coaches following the contest and a heated discussion took place later when the two talked about the final sequence.

You can make the argument that substitute players put in at the end of games want to score and should be allowed to do so. I totally understand that, but there is a right way and a wrong way to finish contests.

I know of one coach who has told me his team will never score 100 points in a game regardless of how inferior the opponent. In blow out victories, he instructs his team to make a certain number of passes before anyone even looks at the basket, because he does not want to run up the score.

I have always been impressed by coaches who tell a quarterback to take a knee outside the goal line in the closing minute of a victory instead of scoring another touchdown. In fact, I have witnessed arguments that have taken place between coaches when just the opposite has occurred and that touchdown was punched in to pad the final margin of victory.

People have long memories when it comes to those types of things. It reminds me of a saying that I heard a long time ago, but it left a lasting impression on me: people may not remember what you said and they may not remember what you did, but they will always remember how you made them feel.

I am at a basketball game one night and the contest is in the waning seconds. The outcome has been decided and the subs are in as the final seconds tick off the clock. A player on the winning team is doing the right thing, holding the ball about 40 feet from the basket.

A fan yells from the stands, "Crank it!"

To which I look over and respond, "No. Why would you do that?"

He says, "Because it might go in."

I respond, "The game is already over."

He says, "Exactly; So, what does it matter?"

I tell him, "That's what leads to hard feelings."

While I believe the fan is well meaning, wanting a JV player to get a three-pointer and get his name in the scorebook, I explain the problem with taking the shot. One, it might indeed go in, so now you're running up the score. Two, even if it doesn't go in, you're still taking the shot which means you're trying to run up the score. Either way, it is not necessary and the bad outweighs the good.

I know this might seem like a small item in the big picture of things, but I believe coaches, players and especially teams develop a reputation for playing the game the right way or playing it the wrong way. If you don't believe me, just ask around and you'll get a quick list of those schools who are known for all the wrong reasons.

It all comes back to the simple fact these are games that kids are playing. They are learning valuable life lessons and there is a lot more to it than simply winning and losing.

07

MEASURE OF SUCCESS

Sports should be about kids and their passion,
not about parents and their goals.
—Mike Matheny

Nearly all parents tend to think their son or daughter is the best player on a team. Some will not admit it, others will readily admit it, but the fact of the matter is, most parents I have dealt with through the years all want their children to be the star player or at the very least play as much if not more than the others on the squad.

If you don't believe me, just go ask a coach sometime what most of his or her discussions are like with parents. I guarantee you it's not about how good of a job the coach is doing.

A while back I had a chat with a highly successful basketball coach. Or what you might think is highly successful. It just depends on who you ask.

A set of parents was not as impressed because their son was not getting the playing time they felt he deserved. The parents proceeded to contact administration and a meeting was held. Following discussions, the parents asked if they could pray for the coach. When they did, the prayer included a request the coach would come to his senses and play their son more.

While I do believe that parents are well intentioned, most of the time they are also unrealistic in their expectations.

In all of my years as a parent of a varsity player, only one time did I have a conversation with a coach about playing time. Isaiah was a seventh grader and had yet to prove he belonged on the varsity tennis team. The coach explained he was probably close to around the 10th or 12th best player on the team. I responded, I thought he was a lot closer to the 7th or 8th best player. That was it. Never brought up again.

I supported the team and my son the best I could the rest of the way. Isaiah ended up proving his worth, eventually climbing as high as No. 6 on the varsity by the time the season was over. Did my conversation have any bearing on that at all? I really hope not, because I wanted Isaiah to earn his position, not have it given to him because his dad planted a suggestion.

Looking back on it, I am not happy to admit my discussion with the coach ever took place. However, I also learned from it and I am hoping others might learn from it as well.

(There's nothing to help a person prepare for the parent trapped within).

Personally, I have a hard time dealing with people who think their son or daughter can do no wrong.

I have had multiple parents tell me, without being prompted, that their son or daughter was among the best players in the state or the conference. For starters, why would I need to know that? Covering sports all my life, if that individual was indeed the best player, it would be obvious. Second, even if those parents were correct in their assessment, what purpose did it serve in telling me that?

I can you tell you exactly the impact it had on me. One, I felt sorry for the players, because their parents felt the need to share that with me. Two, I lost a measure of respect for the parents, because of their arrogance and pride.

According to a recent study, roughly seven percent of all high school athletes go on to play sports in college. Let that sink in for a minute.

Yet, there they are, in one school after another, parents who think their son or daughter is the best player on the team and has a career in athletics ahead of them. I sometimes wonder how coaches are even able to coach at all with all of that amazing talent on their teams.

So where do parents get that notion in the first place?

Well, I can tell you as a parent of an athlete myself, we want more than anything for our child to succeed. I am as guilty of anybody when I say I dreamed of my son making a game-winning shot to win a state championship. There is nothing wrong with that. However, when we become obsessed with individual success over team accomplishments, it becomes a huge problem.

Personally, I think we do our children a huge disservice when we allow them to think they are by far the best player on the team. It leads to more selfish play and less acceptance to take responsibility when things don't go well.

While those issues have likely been around from the inception of sports, I believe we are headed down the wrong path. More and more athletes are encouraged to specialize in one particular sport in order to hone their skills because that's what everybody else is doing.

The best players are targeted as early as elementary school and by the time they reach middle school, the supposed "stars" are on traveling teams and the rest of the kids are discarded by the wayside.

For starters, this is never what sports were intended for; to build all-star teams in hopes of beating other all-star teams and prepping those few select athletes to get ready for the next level. What life lessons are we sending to those who fail to "make the cut," and what are we teaching those who do?

I can name a handful of athletes right off the top of my head who were late bloomers and never even grew into their bodies until late in high school or college. By today's standards, those kids would never even be considered for serious varsity time. Just because you aren't on a high school all-star team doesn't mean you aren't any good. Just because you don't play in a state tournament doesn't mean you don't possess great ability.

I know of two very talented tennis players who thrived in college despite not playing a single point of high school tennis. Jesse Young of Mitchell was a two-time conference player of the year at the University of Sioux Falls and never played in high school. Kyle Jordre of Platte was part of a national championship doubles team at Augustana College despite not playing in high school. Both players benefitted from fathers who were outstanding players, Tom Young and Terry Jordre. But if you went just by the results of the state tennis tourney, Jesse Young and Kyle Jordre wouldn't have even been on the radar screen.

A few years ago, I had a conversation with Britton native Dallas Goedert. He had yet to become a household football name outside of Northeast South Dakota.

He told me during his senior year of high school he was unsure if he was even going to play college football. It would have been easy for him to slip through the cracks. Instead, he ended up walking on at South Dakota State University, worked his tail off and maximized his enormous potential. In 2018, he was drafted by the Philadelphia Eagles and appears to have a huge National Football League career in front of him.

Others use disappointments along the way to fuel their desire to accomplish bigger and better things.

Brock Lesnar was a great athlete in high school. However, during his years at Webster he was unable to win a state championship in wrestling. As a matter of fact, he never even reached the state finals. There was a standout by the name of Brian Van Emmerik of Salem who always stood in his way.

Instead of giving up, Lesnar went into the Marines, emerged bigger and stronger and went on to win a national championship at the University of Minnesota. He then became a prominent name in Ultimate Cage Fighting.

Lesnar, who grew up on a farm, talked about that journey to stardom. He told me once, "I think if I would have won a state title, I wouldn't have had a burning sensation in my heart. I might still be milking cows in Webster if I had beaten Van Emmerik." (American News, Feb. 27, 2005)

Yet, here we are in this day and age, thinking if a player hasn't shown the ability to be the next star player by the time they reach high school, it's not going to happen.

It's certainly a credit to both Goedert and Lesnar that they were able to harness that drive and work ethic in order to reach the top. However, I wonder how many other athletes never even gave it a shot, because they were told at an early age they simply weren't good enough?

We've all heard the story about how Michael Jordan was cut from his high school basketball team and we all know how that turned out.

But I'm afraid the sports landscaped has changed a great deal since then. Many athletes are being encouraged, if not forced, to play a single sport year around. Others simply can't find the time to devote to more than one sport, because of summer camps, open gyms, lifting and the like.

Is it possible for a teenager to be fantastic in more than one sport? Absolutely, and there are many examples of that, like recent Langford Area graduates Chance Olson and Mason Larson. Olson is playing college football and Larson is playing college basketball and each won state track and field championships their senior season of high school. But that is only part of the equation.

Allowing an athlete to participate in more than one sport provides an opportunity to show school spirit, build up different muscle groups and sometimes offer a little lesson in humility as well.

Few things make me happier in sports than when I witness star basketball players who are out for track and field. They might not be gifted runners, but there they are, wearing the school uniform, competing like crazy to support their team. They say fear of failure is a great motivator. But I say those who are willing to risk failure by trying something they are not particularly good at are already proven winners.

And I would bet if you asked the coach of that particular team what that standout athlete in another sport does for the morale of the rest of the members, I think you would find their greatest contribution occurs in the locker room or at practice. Those are some of the life-lessons in sports that never show up in a box score or on a stat sheet.

I applaud those college coaches out there who encourage high schoolers to be multi-sport athletes. They understand there is more to an individual than total touchdowns scored or three-point field goals made.

I'll admit it's somewhat easier to be a multi-sport athlete at small schools, because there are simply not enough players to go around. However, I also believe there is a bit of a stigma when it comes to comparing athletes from larger schools to much smaller schools. Bigger is not always better.

While athletes from the big cities do benefit from better training facilities and better competition, I know of many elite athletes that have come from some of the state's smallest schools.

Daniel Burkhalter is from Prairie City, population 23. (That is not a misprint). More than half the town is made up of his family members. There is one paved road in his town and the closest swimming pool is 45 miles away. Yet, all Burkhalter did is win multiple individual state championships in both cross-country and track and field while competing for Bison High School.

Some of South Dakota's most accomplished athletes from other small towns include Louie Krogman of White River (South Dakota all-time leading scorer for high school boys' basketball), Lincoln McIlravy of Philip (Olympic wrestler), Chad Greenway of Mount Vernon (former linebacker for the Minnesota Vikings), Amanda Madden of Herreid (national champion in the weight throw for Northern State), Riley Reiff of Parkston (current offensive lineman for the Minnesota Vikings), Jesse Bail of Camp Crook (professional saddle bronc rider), Aubrey Baxter of Redfield (national champion in the hammer throw and weight throw for Black Hills State), Bryan Schwartz of Miller (former linebacker for the Jacksonville Jaguars), Jill Young who went to tiny Mitchell Christian (South Dakota all-time leading scorer for high school girls' basketball), Kim Kaufman of Clark (LPGA golfer), Denver TenBroek of McIntosh (former all-time leading scorer for the North Dakota State men's basketball squad), JoEllen Hofer of Hitchcock (who played in back-to-back national championship basketball games for Huron College and Black Hills State), and Macy Heinz of Ipswich (who won a record 19 state track and field championships despite missing her senior season and is now competing for the University of South Dakota).

Those are just a few examples of people who have come from small schools and left their mark on the sports landscape. And the one common denominator: nearly every one of them competed in more than one sport while growing up.

08

GAME DAY

*So often we fail to acknowledge what we have
because we're so concerned about what we want.*
—*John Wooden*

There are few times more exciting in the household of un athlete than game days. Those moments just have a different feel to them, regardless of the sport and regardless of the opponent.

While I have enjoyed covering countless athletes in a variety of venues, it is a bit different when one of your own is in action. It can be a helpless feeling, but one I wouldn't trade for anything. It didn't take me long to figure out I was going to have to learn to control my emotions on this roller-coaster journey of being a sports parent.

It's the second day of the 2013 state tennis tournament. It's a bright sunny afternoon in Brandon. I am settled into my lawn chair as Isaiah is getting ready for consolation action during the tourney. The situation is this: if he wins he continues playing, if he loses his seventh-grade season is over.

He is facing a young man from Huron and things are not going the greatest. In fact, you might say that things are looking pretty bleak. Isaiah is down two match points and the end of the year appears very near. He somehow manages to save both of them and comes back to record a thrilling victory.

Before there is even time to celebrate that win, another match is underway.

This time Isaiah is facing an opponent from Rapid City Central that he defeated about two weeks earlier. Isaiah is doing well and a victory in this match puts into him into the consolation championship the next day.

As my mind begins to drift to his next possible opponent, Isaiah has two match points to finish off his foe. However, in a complete role reversal of his previous match, he loses both of them and ends up losing the match.

I am stunned. His season is over. In a matter of less than 60 minutes my son wins a match he probably should have lost and loses a match he probably should have won. I come the quick realization that if this is the way the next five years are going to play out, I need to be able to control my emotions and expect the unexpected.

(A true picture of the parent trapped within).

Since those early days of his varsity tennis career, my son has been involved in numerous intense battles. He was won some, lost some, played significant roles and played minor roles. I am beyond blessed to say I was there for every single one of those basketball games and tennis matches, home and away, with the exception of one doubles match and I had a very good reason. I was a casketbearer at my uncle's funeral and missed it.

As I stated before, I have never been one to wear my emotions on my sleeve. I have had people ask, how can you stay so calm when your son is out there playing? There are actually several reasons.

Because of my job, I have trained myself to show very little emotion during games. I didn't want to give people the impression I was favoring one team over another in the least little way. I used to plan my wardrobe based on the teams I was covering that week. I would never wear the same colors of the teams I was covering. I also would not sit in a specific team section and I made sure if I stood for one school song I would always stand for the other. Call me paranoid, but I believe that is the best practice. I just cringe at the stuff I witness sometimes when the media member covering the contest could be mistaken as a member of one of the coaching staffs. I actually know of one media member who was cheering so hard for his team while sitting at the scorer's table that he almost cost that team a technical foul.

Another reason I don't show much emotion is because I have seen parents who have crossed the line with their enthusiasm. I vowed I never wanted to called "one of those parents."

You have no idea how tough it can be to hold those feelings inside when your child is involved in a battle for the ages and you just want to let it out. (Really, if anything, that is the genesis of the title for this book). And trust me, there were a few times I couldn't help myself. But for the most part, I just wanted to be there to provide the best support possible and enjoy the ride.

This is what high school athletics is all about. It's a February night in Faulkton and the gym is rocking. Aberdeen Christian and Faulkton are hooked up in a good one and the place is electric. As a sportswriter I used to live for these moments.

With the outcome very much in doubt, there is a timeout called in the final minutes. I look over at my brother, Doug, and say, "Is there any place else you'd rather be right now?"

While tight games might be tough on nerves, when I was covering games I would rather cover a nail-biter than a yawner and even as a parent, I like competitive battles. Although, I must say when you have a child on the floor in a game like this, the pressure is much greater.

The contest comes down to the final seconds and Christian has the ball with a tie score. I get my phone ready to shoot video in case there is a last-second shot. Trey Harms spots Isaiah in the corner outside the three-point line.

Isaiah briefly fumbles the ball, then drives to the basket. Isaiah, all 5-foot-7 of him, shoots over the top of Faulkton's 6-foot-4 center and banks in the shot with just a few seconds remaining. It turns out to be the game-winner and the Aberdeen Christian fans go nuts. It is a night that I will never forget and one that both athlete and parent dream of. I don't end up cheering much, because I am shooting video. I know there will be time to celebrate later.

It would be nice if every game could end similar to that, but I have been around the game long enough to know some athletes and parents will never get to experience that feeling. I understand how meaningful that moment is. And I also know there could be nights ahead where Isaiah has a chance to win a game and misses a shot like that.

The fact of the matter is, parents not only desire their son or daughter make every routine play, but the spectacular ones as well. I have come to realize that is totally unrealistic. No matter how talented individuals are, they are also human and they make mistakes. That is a simple fact of life. Yet is also a hard lesson to learn.

There were many occasions where I found myself cringing as Isaiah would throw the ball away or miss an easy shot. That is where Lauretta would always be the voice of reason. "I'm sure he's doing the best he can," she would say. That did little to console me, but I also knew she was right.

It's Parents Day Isaiah's senior season. Aberdeen Christian is playing Waubay-Summit. While the Mustangs are struggling, I also know they have one of the best coaches in the game on their bench in Mark Amdahl. Not only is Mark an outstanding coach, but a long-time friend. I have watched him go from a rookie head coach trying to find his way to a veteran head coach with multiple state championships in girls' basketball to his credit.

It is one of those days where Isaiah is having a hard time making a shot. In fact, he misses all three of his free-throw attempts in the contest for maybe the only time in his career. (This from a person who is a former state free-throw shooting champion who once made 10 free throws in a row during a varsity contest.) Christian wins the game, but I am not overly pleased.

I visit with Coach Amdahl following the contest. He says his halftime speech revolved around stopping Andrew Rohrbach and Isaiah. I almost laugh out loud and say, "Isaiah couldn't even make a free throw today."

Coach Amdahl responds by saying, "He's a good player. I'd sure take him on my team."

I am not looking for a compliment, but I must admit, it feels good to hear that. And it also makes me realize that maybe as a parent I see all of the flaws and ignore some of the positives.

(Sometimes parents view things differently than anyone else).

Fans and to a certain degree media are focused on who scores the touchdowns, who makes the points, who hits the home runs. We are trained to think that way, because that is who draws the headlines, who garners the post-game interviews.

However, I have also trained myself to look at the game-within-the-game. I pay close attention to who is throwing the block to spring the big run. Who is setting the pick to free up the shooter. Who is denying the post feed or fighting through the screen to prevent a wide-open look.

I've always tried to give credit where credit is due, even when it is not obvious to the casual observer.

Sometimes, though, that perspective can get warped when you are watching your own son, for better or worse.

It's another intense contest. This time the foe is Potter County. I've always said there is no more fitting mascot for a team than the Battlers, because they bring it every night and battle until the end.

This evening is no different. Christian is ahead the whole game but cannot shake the Battlers. This one is going to come down to the final shot and Potter County will take it.

Again, the media training in me has me primed to shoot video of the final seconds. Imagine trying to be a parent and still being somewhat objective in that moment.

(It's never easy being the parent trapped within).

The Battlers run their best player off a series of screens, but his shot is contested and falls off the rim at the final horn. Christian wins a nail-biter and I exhale knowing the squad has dodged a bullet, but pleased at knowing the Knights beat a very solid team.

Later that night, we talk about the play around the dining room table. I say that was a good defensive stand at the end. Isaiah begins to tell me how hard he worked to get through screens to make sure he could contest the final shot. I am startled.

I say, "Was that you? I have it here on video tape. Let me watch it."

Sure enough. As I replay the sequence, there it is. Isaiah, the smallest player on the floor, fighting through screens to contest a much taller opponent on his potential game-winning shot. I am proud of his effort and I am embarrassed I was so into the game I failed to realize it was my own son who had helped to preserve the victory.

Through it all, there are so many life lessons to be learned through athletics. I used to think they were all to be learned by the athletes. However, this little journey as a parent of an athlete has shown me that there are just as many lessons to be learned by parents like me as well. I just had to open my eyes and my mind to see those opportunities and benefit from them.

STATISTICS

Don't let talent get in way of team performance.
Great players do what's outstanding for team,
not what makes them stand out.
—Jerry West

They always say numbers tell the story. Well, it's been my experience that sometimes numbers only tell part of the story and sometimes numbers can be very misleading.

However, in today's world of sports, we have become consumed by numbers. Just watch a professional game of any kind and you will find out way more information about a player than you ever wanted to know. It seems like there are numbers for how many times a particular batter has hit a lead-off home run on artificial turf against a left-handed pitcher with his team trailing after the fourth inning. Really? Who keeps those kinds of records?

That said, I believe there is too great of an emphasis on numbers. I totally understand we use those numbers to measure success, but too often those numbers can lead to selfish play. I have witnessed it far more often than once.

We now live in a time where organizations and certain members of the media are predicting on social media how many points or touchdowns a certain high school player will score against an opponent. I can't imagine that this trend will help team unity in the long run. If anything, it could lead to more selfish play and teams running up the score.

And while the players are the ones who are racking up the numbers, it is the coaches who are enabling them to do it. I have seen a coach leave his star player in a game with a minute remaining, up 30 points. Worse yet, that player is jacking up three-point shots. I once saw a coach pull his starters in a lopsided contest with five minutes left only to reinsert them two minutes later to pad their stats.

There was one coach who force-fed a player against lesser opponents in blowout victories just so he would be able to reach the 1,000-point plateau before his career ended. I am not sure how that helped anybody. It's certainly not what athletics are intended for.

I know of another school which combined a player's varsity and junior varsity points so that a certain player could reach 1,000 points. Those records should not count.

So why all the fanfare about points anyway? There have always been big scorers. You can go back to the 1940s and 1950s and find guys who scored more than 1,000 career points. While they did not have the three-point line of today, they also played up to 35 or 40 games in a season.

The difference was those players did not live in the era of social media. Games couldn't be watched on the internet and people weren't consumed by numbers.

Doug Schlepp was a standout player who graduated from Java High School in 1970. He went on to score more than 2,400 points in college at South Dakota School of Mines. I asked him how many points he scored in high school and he didn't know. The school closed, the records were lost and nobody seems to have them. It certainly didn't make him any less of a player. Here's his take on the issue:

"I have no idea what happened to those records and was never able to track it down. And I guess I never saw the need to necessarily track it down." (The Legends Sports Show, Feb. 1, 2018)

Cary Hornaman, in my opinion, is the greatest player ever to come out of Aberdeen Roncalli. He recently had his career scoring mark broken. The most interesting part of that story is Cary didn't even know he owned the record dating back to the mid 1970s. Back then, people weren't totally enamored with statistics. They played for the love of the game.

This is what Cary said about his scoring record that stood for more than 40 years:

"For a while I didn't even know I still had it. They never talked about thousand-point scorers. I didn't even know how many points I had." (The Legends Sports Show, Jan. 18, 2018)

I often wonder how games would look if the only statistic kept was the final score. Instead, we now have scoreboards that feature individual statistics for each player on the court. I have actually seen players look up at those during the course of a game. I really hope it's not to see how many points they have accumulated.

It's a Friday afternoon consolation game during a state basketball tournament. Nothing out of the ordinary in what is known as the "sunshine bracket."

The game I happen to be covering does not feature much drama. One team is handing it to the other. The real drama takes place after the game.

As I interview the winning coach, he takes exception with me for not telling him his star player was close to breaking a tournament record for most points scored in a consolation game. I am stunned.

For starters, it isn't my job to tell a coach his player is close to breaking a record. Second, I would not have told him even if I knew he was close to a record, especially since that team had the game well in hand anyway. I think to myself, does that record mean that much to you that you are willing to kick a little more dirt into your opponent's face?

In the 2017-2018 season, there were 1,000-point scorers all over the place in South Dakota high school basketball (including two who reached the milestone in the same game). There were some 1,000-point scorers back in my day as well, but they certainly weren't as prominent as they are today. The three-point line and the shot clock have undoubtedly led to higher-scoring games. (Although I would argue that the shot clock does not necessarily mean more points, only more bad shots taken because offenses now have to shoot the ball quicker. I believe it rewards good defensive teams because they only have to defend hard for 35 seconds).

So, does scoring 1,000 points make you a selfish player? Not hardly. But it does tell you something about today's mindset when so much emphasis is placed on that milestone compared to generations past. It all comes back to being a team player and what you are doing to make your teammates better. It certainly is possible to be a big-time scorer and a great team leader. There are countless examples of that. However, it's also possible to pad your stats and not be a team-first player.

Like I said earlier in this chapter, sometimes numbers can be very misleading. During my newspaper career, I helped to select the All-Area football and basketball teams recognizing the top high school players in the coverage area. I would contact coaches from various conferences to help ensure we picked the most deserving players possible. Of course, numbers would invariably play a role in the process, but I can honestly tell you that numbers weren't the end all that people think.

I recall a football coach nominating two players from his team with numbers that caught my attention. I began to think about those numbers in relation to his team's success that year. I did a little further checking and realized his team was only about .500 and missed the playoffs. It made me think the numbers those players had did not matchup with what happened on the field.

I made a few more phone calls and realized that the coach was telling the truth, but that the truth was very misleading. Those players did indeed have nice statistics, but they were racking up major yards in blowout losses after the opponents had put in their second or third string units. Those players did very little against starting defenses.

On the other hand, I know full well there are good players who are limited by the teams they play for. That's one of the main reasons why I would call as many coaches as possible to find that "diamond in the rough." Each year, I was able to discover that player or two that was stuck on a bad team and never garnered much attention, but yet still deserved to be named to the All Area team.

When opposing coaches would say, "The team wasn't very good, but we couldn't stop that guy," that made me believe he was a formidable player. In those cases, numbers had very little to do with it.

Of course, if we didn't have numbers what would we talk about when it comes to sports? Fantasy football leagues would shut down in a heartbeat. Betting lines would dry up. People would lose millions and millions of dollars. Hmm. Is that what we've become as a society? Can't just watch a game for the sake of good plays, or seeing players come together as one unit and produce an improbable victory?

And don't kid yourself to think that gambling is confined to boxing, horse racing or professional sports. It's not. I once had a person tell me about an individual who was betting on high school athletics. The addiction was so bad he eventually lost all he had on the outcome of a contest featuring teenage boys and was forced to relocate to a different part of the state. Sad.

There is no doubt in my mind we have become who we are because of the times we live in. While there have always been issues connected with sports, there was always a bit of an innocence when it came to high school games. Each year, that innocence erodes a little bit more and a little bit more.

There are plenty of places to blame, but I would put social media right at the top. In this day of YouTube videos, Hudl, and many other sites, people are trying to out-do each other for the most unbelievable play. I call it the SportsCenter mentality. If players can make a spectacular play, why would they settle for the fundamentally correct one?

As a result, in some instances skills are eroding and in other cases good judgment certainly is. I have seen players try to make a highlight-reel pass that sometimes ends halfway up the bleachers, instead of making the right pass that would lead to a layup. And how can you blame today's teens when their idols in the NBA are doing the exact same thing?

We've likely all seen professionals pass up dunks to kick it out to the wing for three-point shots. Who teaches that philosophy? The problem is, today's stars make the game look so easy, they can often get away with it.

And sometimes the law of averages catchup with even some of the best players in the world. In the 2018 NBA playoffs the Houston Rockets missed a mind-numbing 27 three-point shots in a row during one playoff game.

It's a trend we are seeing more often in today's sports: go big or go home. It's why home runs are up in major league baseball and people are willing to look the other way as strikeouts soar as well. (This past year marked the first time in history that there were more strikeouts than hits in major league baseball). It is why power running backs are becoming more and more devalued in the National Football League as teams are looking to hit the big strike and play a more wide-open style of offense.

Are those bad things? Not for entertainment value, but it certainly goes against conventional coaching wisdom and can also produce bad habits for today's younger generation.

Not only that, but social media can certainly lead to competition between teammates, whether intentional or not. While parents can be well meaning, I believe posting everything their son or daughter does on Facebook or Twitter is not always the most positive thing. At its worst, it can lead to jealousy among other parents; at its best it can produce the perception of pride and arrogance. There's nothing wrong with celebrating a major accomplishment, but to constantly dote on your child is not healthy for anybody.

10

FANFARE

*The most valuable player is the one that
makes the most players valuable.*
—Peyton Manning

I've seen parents handle stressful situations in a variety of ways through the years. Some scream, some wrinkle up their programs, some chew their nails. And then there is Darrin Smith of Sioux Falls.

I got to know Darrin a long time ago when our sons played against each other in a youth tennis tournament in Pierre. Because our sons are the same age, our paths crossed annually if not more often.

Darrin traveled all across the state to watch his son play tennis. The only problem was, Darrin often couldn't handle watching his son play tennis.

It's a Saturday afternoon in April 2017. I am sitting in the bleachers in Aberdeen watching Isaiah play a doubles match against Yankton in the annual Rezatto Rumble, a tournament featuring teams from across the state. I sense somebody over my right shoulder watching the action as well. I glance over and it's Darrin.

"Hey Darrin, isn't Spenser playing right now?" I ask, wondering why he is watching my son instead of his.

"Yeah, he's back there," Darrin says, pointing to a court behind us.

My immediate thought is, why did you drive 200 miles to watch somebody else's son play instead of yours?

"Well, why aren't you watching him?" I ask.

"Oh, I can't take it," Darrin replies.

I believe he initially means his son's doubles team is not fairing too well. While that may have caused him to leave, there appears to be something else at play. I look over and see the team is making a comeback. I encourage him to go back over and watch, but then realize a little superstition could be involved, when he says maybe staying away is a good thing because they are making a comeback.

As Isaiah's doubles match finishes, I encourage Darrin to head back over to watch Spenser finish up his match. This is just one of many occasions where Spenser Smith plays and his father is off in the distance keeping a watchful eye on the action, but seldom next to the court.

Now, I have seen just the opposite happen as well. In fact, I am probably part of that delegation. The one who never misses a match and would sit on the court if you let him. I often found the best seat in the house to watch a match.

Not Darrin Smith. If Spenser was playing, there was a good chance Darrin was in the area code, even though I had a hard time spotting him, but definitely not front and center. It didn't matter if the match took place in Watertown or Sioux Falls, the scenario was always the same.

The 2017 State Tennis Tournament is nearing the end of its opening day. As my wife and I watch a doubles match at McKennan Park in Sioux Falls, I spot Darrin about a half a block away walking back and forth. That meant one thing: Spenser was playing close by.

Sure enough, I take a quick peek behind me and my suspicions are confirmed. Spenser and his partner are playing on the court right behind us. Darrin may not have been courtside, but he knew full well what was going on.

Watching a child participate in any sport can be difficult. You want your children to do well and play up to their potential, but you cannot do anything to help them. (In all honesty, I have learned at that particular moment they really don't want your help anyway. Afterall, it really is their battle, not yours).

I have talked to several tennis parents who described the experience of watching their sons play tennis. They talk about finding it difficult to breath and gut-wrenching. While I wouldn't want to miss the experience, it can be anything but peaceful and relaxing.

(That might be the best definition of the parent trapped within).

I came across Darrin again last spring. I was a bit surprised to see him next to the court watching Spenser play his matches.

"I'm over it," Darrin assures me. "I've learned how to handle it now."

We share a good laugh over it and prepare for the following week's state tournament in Rapid City.

It's late Friday afternoon at the 2018 state tourney in Rapid City, and Sioux Falls Roosevelt is playing Sioux Falls Lincoln in the semifinals at first flight doubles. The match is tight, the points are dynamic and the atmosphere is electric.

There are probably close to 100 people lined up behind the baseline three and four rows deep. As I watch the match play out, I look around and notice that there is one person in particular that is noticeably absent. There is no Darrin Smith in sight.

The match finally concludes with Roosevelt pulling out a victory. About 20 minutes later, I stumble across Darrin.

"Darrin, where were you?" I ask. "That was a great match."

"I couldn't do it," he says.

He explains he walked back and forth to the nearest sub shop about six blocks away (twice).

"I thought about you," Darrin says, knowing what he had told me a week earlier.

Not that Darrin ever has to answer to me. But I wonder how he can possibly drive more than 300 miles one way and miss one of his son's biggest matches ever.

"Weren't you curious how the match was going?" I ask.

He tells me he knew it was close and somebody would text him updates.

Because of the outcome of that match, it meant Spenser and his partner would play in the doubles championship the next day. I ask if he would be in attendance watching that match.

"Oh, I'll be here for that," Darrin promises. "I'll put my house on that."

As it turns out, Spenser plays in the state championship match in both singles and doubles, and true to his word, Darrin is right next to the fence watching every point.

Sometimes parents are pulled in two different directions making it impossible to watch multiple children. During the basketball season, especially in Class AA schools, girls and boys often play at the same time in two different cities.

I once asked a parent who had a son and a daughter playing at the same time in two different towns how he decided which one to watch. He said he and his wife came up with the answer before the season started: they would watch whichever one happened to be in town that evening.

I know others who decided to watch whichever child was a senior, figuring that would be their last chance while the other child would have more games in the future.

Thanks to technology today, the internet makes following multiple children much easier. I have been at games where a husband and wife were watching one child in front of them on the court while keeping an eye on another child (playing in a different city) on a laptop computer set up in front of them on the bleachers.

Of course, state tennis can provide a whole different set of circumstances.

Because not all of the matches can be played at one bank of courts, sometimes brothers or sisters are split up, playing at the same time at two different locations in the same city.

That was the case at the 2018 state tournament for Lee and Peg Goetz, whose sons Lucas and Joseph played for Aberdeen Roncalli. On the second day of the state tournament, the two sons played at different venues at approximately the same time.

It's about lunch time and Lucas and Isaiah are just finishing up their singles matches at Parkview in Rapid City. They have a doubles match coming up shortly and a group of us, including Lee, decide to grab a quick bite to eat.

However, the atmosphere at lunch is a bit distracting because Joseph is playing in a close match across town over at Sioux Park. While Peg is there, Lee can only get updates as his son is playing in one of the biggest matches of his life.

"Aren't you nervous?" I ask as we sit down to eat.

"Not really. There's nothing I can do," says Lee.

Personally, I know I would not be able to eat at all, let alone enjoy my food, if my son was in the same situation.

We continue to get updates and Lee is as calm as can be. He either has ice in his veins or is an incredibly good actor.

The updates indicate Joseph is ahead, but the match is tight. We get a text that says Joseph is up a set and leads a tiebreaker 5-0. All is well, until the updates stop coming.

"What is taking so long? What's going on with the match?" says Lee, who is now understandably starting to get a bit anxious.

We finally get word Joseph has won and moved into the next day's semifinals.

Lee gives me a high-five slap that hits my hand so hard my fingers literally tingle for 10 seconds after.

It's hard being a tennis parent.

(And it can be hard being the parent trapped within).

Watching children compete in any extra-curricular activity can be a fun, yet stressful situation. During a concert you hope they don't come in at the wrong time and sing out of place. During a team sport, you hope they don't commit a penalty that will wipe out a touchdown. However, individual sports like tennis or wrestling can take that stress mode to a whole different level.

And unless you experience it firsthand, you simply have no idea what it feels like watching a son or a daughter compete, especially in a state tournament atmosphere.

That parent perspective was driven home during the semifinals of the 2018 state tennis tournament.

Because of rain, the matches are moved indoors. The seating is limited, but it sure beats the alternative of not being able to play.

As Joseph Goetz plays his match, a group of Roncalli players and parents watch the match from upstairs at the Black Hills Tennis Center. The match is close and eventually heads to a super tiebreaker to determine which player will go on to play for the state championship at flight three singles later in the day.

"Oh man, I hate this," says Roncalli senior player Austin Kokales as he watches the event unfold along with the rest of us.

He then turns and looks at the parents.

"Is this how you guys feel all the time?" he asks.

Bingo!

Now, I realize that stressing out while watching your son or daughter will do nothing to help the situation. In fact, often it compounds the matter, because they can sense through your body language what you might be thinking.

However, given the choice of which one I would rather do, watching an event involving one of my children or watching somebody else, I would prefer having one of my kids participating, even if it is more stressful. Not that they are assured of success and not that I know what will happen in that particular activity. But there is just something very rewarding knowing your son or daughter is out there competing, learning life lessons and hopefully building memories that will last a lifetime.

11

CULTURE

If you're not making mistakes, then you're not doing anything.
I'm positive that a doer makes mistakes.
—*John Wooden*

I'm not sure what sports used to be like years and years ago, but I sure know what they have turned into in this day and age.

I believe sports used to be more of a diversion, an escape from the trials and tribulations of real-life issues. While still featuring an entertainment aspect, sports has evolved into much, much more today.

There are now multiple stations that broadcast solely sports programming 24 hours a day. When I was growing up, we all waited for the Saturday Major League Baseball Game of the Week. Now, you can have your choice of any game that you want. While there have always been "experts" in the stands, I believe with the advancement of technology, more people are exposed to more games and there are even more "experts" in the stands today. And that has trickled down to high school athletics, predominantly parents.

While there have always been arm-chair quarterbacks who second guess everything from the calls of umpires to the play calls of coaches, I think parents feel more emboldened and empowered to voice their opinions than ever before.

The problem is the game, at least at the high school level, is not intended to be about those in the stands. It is for the players and those with something at stake.

This can be a very difficult lesson to learn for parents, myself included. Maybe it's the media member in me, but I'm afraid it's more of the competitor in me for the reason I tend get too involved.

I have found myself trying to figure out seed points for my son's basketball team. Not just a little figuring, but actually armed with a calculator penciling out possible playoff scenarios with totals down to percentage points. While there is no harm in doing that, in actuality, what did it really matter to me? I wasn't playing in the game and I couldn't change the outcome of the matchups, either.

For whatever reason, either too busy, lesson learned, whatever, in 2018 I did not tabulate seed points for tennis. While I was curious where Isaiah would land, I did not lose sleep over it nor did I rack my brain trying to figure out the possible scenarios. However, I do know of some parents who could even tell you their theories on who might be ducking who in order to maximize seed positioning for the state tournament. You might have wondered if the parents themselves were planning on playing the matches. (I would probably actually pay to see that).

Even knowing the results of the game should never mean more to the parents than the athletes, I can attest it is difficult to remember that lesson during the heat of the moment.

It is the conclusion of a long day of tennis in Rapid City. The results of the afternoon are mixed and as we head out to supper, I am frustrated that Isaiah did not play up to his potential.

As we sit around the table on the outdoor patio, the beauty of the Black Hills provides a scenic backdrop to our meal. The mood around me is jovial. The other

Roncalli parents are talking about the NFL Draft currently underway on the TV screen.

Meanwhile, I am doing a slow boil. I am still not over the fact Isaiah and his partner lost a match they should have won. (Like it really should make a difference to me).

I glance down to the other end of the table and the Roncalli players are laughing and having a great time. They have moved on. I think to myself, what is wrong with this picture? Why should I be upset and they be able to relax and forget about it?

Then I think about what I try to preach to everybody else: the parent should never want it worse than the athlete.

(If only I could figure out what do with the parent trapped within).

If there is one thing I do know it's that kids are much more resilient than adults give them credit for.

While teenagers compete like crazy, get frustrated when things don't go their way on occasion, and all want to experience success, for the most part they treat the game for what it is: a game. Most of the biggest rivalries I have covered through the years have more to do with the parents than the players involved. Sometimes the players will even go out together after a game while the parents will sit and stew over the results.

So why is it parents make more out of games than they should?

Part of it is pride. They simply don't want to lose to a certain team or a particular opponent. How on earth will they face their co-workers around the water cooler?

Part of it is selfishness. How could my son or daughter do this me? Don't they know my sports legacy? Don't they know how much this means to me?

Now, I totally understand we celebrate our children's accomplishments and we lament their shortcomings. It's all part of being a family. Something would be horribly wrong if we took joy in our children's failures or felt jealous of their success.

The problem is too often adults (parents as well as coaches) put far too great of emphasis on winning instead of effort. Not everybody is going to win a championship even though everybody wants to.

I am walking through a store and encounter the parent of an athlete a couple of weeks after a state wrestling tournament. The look on his face says it all.

His son, one of the state's elite wrestlers, got upset in his quest for a state championship. I'm not sure what the status of the son is, but the mood of the parent is borderline depression.

We chat for a while and he tells me his son's defeat in the state tourney, "feels like there is a death in the family."

(I want you to stop reading for a few seconds and let that sink in.)

I assure him his son will be just fine. That he is still a quality wrestler and sometimes things just don't work out like we want.

I know the hurt is real. In fact, if athletes do not feel downtrodden or even shed a tear or two, then there is probably something wrong. It shows how much they have invested in their activity. It may even linger for a short while and in some cases serve as motivation for future seasons.

However, when parents still struggle to come to grips with a loss a few weeks after the fact, there's a chance that they were a bit too invested in the first place.

Again, I totally get this. As a competitor myself, I don't like losing. Especially when I feel like I was the better player or I did not play up to my potential. But those are the events that involve me, not my children. When I start caring about their games and competitions more than they do, it indicates one of two things: they aren't as invested as they should be or I am involved way more than I should be.

Now, there are rare moments where parents aren't nearly as involved in their kids' activities as they should be. I have gone to home games and wondered where some of the players' parents were at. I can understand the unwillingness to travel to road games, but time after time not showing up for home games? What message is that sending to their children?

As a parent, there is a fine line between caring too much and giving the appearance of not caring at all. Sometimes it can be a difficult lesson to learn.

I do know one fact, the last thing an athlete needs or desires after a contest is a parent who critiques the performance. It doesn't matter if that advice is well intentioned or not.

Wayne Carney, former Executive Director for the South Dakota High School Activities Association, once told me there's only three things you should ask your athlete following a contest: 1, Did you have fun? 2, What did you learn? 3, Where do you want to eat?

There's a lot of truth in that philosophy.

I talked to one parent who said he always waited for at least 24 hours before he would discuss an event his children competed in.

My personal approach was to be very delicate and often let our kids bring up the event first. I would always try to stay as positive as possible, even if I did not feel it was their best effort. And I am convinced my kids would tell you sometimes I failed in this quest.

What parents need to realize is at the very foundation, those who are involved in extra-curricular activities in the first place are to be applauded. They are not sitting at home on a couch playing a video game or on their cell phones 24-7. They may not be the star players. They may not even be the best role players, but the fact of the matter is, they are willing to risk failure because they are willing to participate. You cannot win if you do not play. And sometimes it doesn't matter if you win or not.

Somewhere along the line, that connection has been lost. It has turned into who has the best scoring average, who made the all-star team, who has the most YouTube highlight plays?

I often ask coaches on my shows how do you measure success? Is it beating the opponent you are facing, is it beating your personal best performance, it is showing week-to-week improvement throughout the course of the season?

The most successful coaches I have dealt with through the years tell me they very seldom talk about winning and losing. They talk about the two things everybody can control: attitude and effort. They talk about doing the little things right. If athletes do those things, the end result is usually success on the scoreboard. And if it isn't, the end result is definitely success in the effort. And at the end of the day, what more could a coach or a parent ask for?

PARENTING CHECKLIST

❏ Sometimes parents see all of the flaws and ignore some of the positives.

❏ The parent should never want it worse than the athlete.

❏ Parents need to remain positive, understanding and supportive through the peaks and valley of athletics.

❏ Some parents are far more determined to achieve what they believe to be success than the athletes and coaches. That is a major problem.

❏ Athletics are your child's own personal journey, not yours as a parent.

❏ If your measure of success has anything to do with state championships, wins or personal statistics, prepare yourself for disappointment and heartache.

❏ Allow your son or daughter to share the joys and frustrations of athletic events without letting your own opinions take over the conversation.

❏ If you are feeling responsible for your child's success and happiness in athletics, bad things will happen.

❏ Value the journey more than the results.

❏ Don't take these years for granted. They promise to be the most eventful, stress-filled, unpredictable, joyous, meaningful and rewarding times of your life.

12

ENTITLEMENT

Developing better people should be the number one goal
for any coach when dealing with kids.
—Bobby Orr

We live in a day and age where people are constantly shouting over the top of everybody else just to have their voices heard. I remember back in the day when announcers just talked in a normal voice. Now, people doing play-by-play of contests or talk radio shout and scream even when they don't need to.

I once had the privilege to have a nice personal visit with the late Jim Simpson. You might recall Jim was a standout announcer back in the 1970s and 1980s for NBC and later ESPN. I still have games on VHS tapes where he was the lead announcer. He talked about the days when people didn't have to shout to be heard.

While there have always been loud and boisterous fans, we have evolved to the point where no matter how big or small the venue and no matter how many people are in attendance, it seems we are bombarded with noise and commotion non-stop. There is a reason for this trend.

There have been studies done that show our attention spans are becoming shorter and shorter. We are nearing the point where we crave constant stimulus. Go to a ball game at nearly any level these days and watch all of the activity during a stoppage in play. I remember the last time I attended an NBA game. I was actually more entertained during the timeouts than I was when the game was in motion.

So what impact if any does this have on parents of players? Personally, I believe it emboldens more and more people to shout at the coaches, shout at the refs and unfortunately, shout at the athletes competing. Think about it. If you are a mild-mannered parent and you see those around you exhibiting boisterous behavior, are you not at least tempted to join in the fray? I know on a personal level it has had a bit of an affect on me.

Again, recall that I consider myself to be a very laidback fan who tries his best to stay calm no matter what the circumstances. You might recall from a previous chapter that I have had individuals ask me, how do you remain so emotionless when your son is playing? Trust me, sometimes it does not come easy, but I have found for the most part it is the right, if not necessarily the natural thing, to do.

Of course, it's difficult in a sport like tennis where there are few fans around to drown out my actions.

The tennis dual against Watertown is coming down to the final match. Isaiah is hooked up in a battle and I have a front row seat. It is only natural for a parent to applaud after a good shot or readjust in a chair after a bad one. While I do not think I am doing anything out of the ordinary apparently, I am wrong.

During a changeover, I offer a bit of support/advice to Isaiah who is not having any of it. The exchange is anything but cordial. The gist of the conservation is he tells me it would help if I would stop making negative gestures any time he makes an error. I tell him to stop watching me and concentrate on the match.

Do you know how difficult it is to do your best mannequin impersonation while an intense match involving your son plays out right in front of you?

(It can be extremely difficult dealing with the parent trapped within).

That is the thing about tennis. It is a quiet sport so any sort of comment or gesture is magnified about 10 times compared to basketball or other sports. There is a certain etiquette at play.

Unlike basketball where fans applaud missed shots and turnovers, football where spectators cheer about fumbles, or volleyball where people cheer when an opponent hits a ball into the net, tennis is a sport where for the most part people do not celebrate another player's mistake.

However, because fans are so close to the action and because there are a lot of quiet moments in tennis, comments can be easily understood and it's easy to tell who is saying them. That in itself can be problematic. A larger crowd in a big venue can be much more forgiving than an intimate tennis setting.

There were times when all I would say is, "Come on, let's get this one right here," and it would initiate a response from Isaiah like I had yelled at the top of my lungs. One time he looked over and put his finger in front of his mouth to shush me.

I know I am not the only parent who has been told to keep quiet during a match, even though my actions are a bit tame compared to others I have witnessed and others I have heard about.

During a match a while back, a former tennis mom says her husband used to get on her son while he was playing. Naturally, the son did not approve so the dad promised not to say anything at the matches anymore.

As the story goes, while the son was playing a match, the dad could not hold back his feelings. While standing next to a school official, he hollered at his son to move his feet.

The mom says the son put down his racquet, came over to the fence and told his father to shut up right in front of the school official.

The mom says, "Now I had to go home and be the mediator. I had to reprimand my son for being disrespectful to his father in front of a school official and I had to reprimand my husband for breaking his promise to our son."

If anybody thinks it is easy being a parent of an athlete in any sport, think again.

Personally, I think being a tennis parent might actually be tougher than those of other sports, for a couple of reasons.

First, tennis is one of those rare sports where the players are on the honor system. There are no officials to call whether the ball is in or out (except for state championship matches). Players are instructed to be honest and to say the score before every point. While most of the time there are few issues, it only takes one perceived bad call to change the entire atmosphere of a match.

I have seen tempers flare, the environment become hostile and words exchanged over just one call. And to be totally fair about this, there are probably 3-4 instances in nearly every match where there is a point that ends on a questionable call. Sometimes you catch a break and sometimes you don't. And there are times when a player hits a ball so hard, it's difficult to tell if it's in or out either way.

Players are always instructed that unless they see a ball as clearly out, they have to play it as being in. That does not prevent the occasional call which cannot only get inside the head of a player, but completely turn the match around on a dime. For that reason alone, I always prayed Isaiah would never be involved in a controversial call that would impact a match.

Another reason being a tennis parent is difficult is because of the drama and intensity that mounts on each passing point. There are stressful moments in every sport, but most other events feature a score clock and those moments are resolved in a relatively short period of time. Not tennis.

Because there is no clock, tennis matches can go on for long stretches and the tension often intensifies as the action continues. It's kind of like seeing a storm moving in and not being able to do anything about it as the clouds darken and the wind picks up. As a spectator you can feel the tension building up and there is no release valve. And really, no way to alleviate that pressure inside of you either, because unlike other sports you are not permitted to holler and scream.

Through nearly four decades of covering sporting events, I have seen my share of intense moments. I have worked games involving multiple overtimes. I have been front row at some of the most heated rivalries. In reality, only a handful of those emotionally charged events have involved my children, but I can tell you this, I have never had my stomach turn into a knot like it has during a tennis match.

I have a strong hunch I am not alone in my feelings about this. I know for a fact Isaiah said tennis featured a lot more pressure and stress than playing basketball.

Again, there is a huge life-long lesson in this and not only for the players involved. How do the coaches and the parents react during those tense moments and how do they conduct themselves when things don't turn out the way they want?

I have seen coaches get into arguments with each other. I have witnessed parental behavior that is unacceptable. And at the end of the day, what lessons are we teaching the teenagers who are involved in playing sports? Is the game becoming too important? Is it OK to carry a grudge against a person because of a perceived bad call that was probably accurate in the first place?

I have always tried to cut the athletes a little slack for their lack of judgement when it comes to behavior, comments or ability. They are teenagers who are just trying to find their way through life. You expect them to make some mistakes along the way.

I tend to be a lot less understanding when it comes to adults who should know better. Do we all make mistakes, regardless of our age? Absolutely, but we also need to know impressionable young people are watching and often emulating our behavior. Changing the culture is a huge task, but it starts one person at a time and we can make a difference if we are willing to be good role models.

Sometimes it can be what we say, like providing words of encouragement to the athletes and coaches. Other times it can be what we don't say, like refraining from criticizing the coach, the official and the participants. I know high school sports play a huge role in our society. Just try not to make the outcomes more important than they really are.

13

SETTING THE TONE

Don't ever permit the pressure to exceed the pleasure.
That's on the top of my lineup card every night.
—Joe Maddon

There are no shortcuts to success. It doesn't matter what sport you play hard work and sacrifice are just part of the process. That's why I like the saying that "the only place success comes before work is in the dictionary."

It has been my experience that teams which do not possess a physical presence will likely have difficulty winning significant games. Athletes need to be the hammer and not the nail. I have seen superior athletes lose games because they could not match the intimidation or physical nature of an opposing foe. Part of that equation is mental and obviously part of it is physical.

I am not opposed to coaches who push their players. It's really hard to reach maximum potential unless somebody or something does push you. However, sometimes it's difficult to tell when push comes to shove.

If there is one thing I have found to be true through the years is when the stakes begin to rise so does the intensity and the aggressiveness. It's kind of like an animal trapped in a corner. Desperate times call for desperate measures.

Therein lies the genesis of a potential problem. Players tend to push and shove a little harder, coaches scream a little louder and fans act a little crazier. Add them to together and it suddenly becomes a recipe for a time bomb. It is most definitely not an atmosphere for the weak of heart.

I have been in wrestling rooms at late-season practices and I swear boot camp with the Marines would be a little less demanding. The intensity can reach fever pitch and keep in mind, this is just practice. There is little room for compassion or sympathy at some of these practices. And it definitely carries over to matches.

Trust me, if a wrestler knows his opponent has one slight weakness, whether it be physical injury or a fragile mentality, he becomes like a shark smelling blood in the water. There is no backing off.

It should come as no surprise that as athletes and coaches get their game-faces on, so do the fans.

It's a cold, snowy Saturday and the Webster Armory is packed full of rabid wrestling fans for this region tournament. To say there is a lot at stake would be a huge understatement. The top place-winners from here advance to the state tournament, the others are done for the season.

I am on assignment with camera around my neck and notebook in hand. I am standing next to a mat getting ready to shoot a photo when I realize I am in the combat zone.

"Break his arm off, Jesse!," a man shouts, "Just break it off!"

I glance to my left and there he is, the wrestler's dad not far away from me. His jugular vein is sticking out and his eyes look like saucers. I slowly back away from the action not wanting to get within his line of sight.

I guarantee you this is not an isolated situation. In fact, I think it might be more like the norm. Now, there is nothing wrong with a little enthusiasm for your favorite competitor. I also know that to be heard in a loud gym you have to strain your vocal chords just a bit. However, it can be pretty easy to lose control of your emotions in that kind of an environment.

Wrestling is a unique sport in that it really involves a person's manhood. It pits one person against another and nobody wants to walk off the mat feeling like he is the weaker of the two. It can turn personal in a big hurry. And believe me when I say, that wrestling fans are some of the most passionate, loyal and knowledgeable fans of their sport of anybody I have ever come across. There are times when casual fans will show up at a basketball or football game, but not at wrestling. Fans that attend wrestling matches come with a purpose.

Intense fan behavior crosses over a multitude of sports and does not have to be limited to the postseason, either. In fact, contests involving two rivals can also bring out the best in people and the worst in people. That same love-hate relationship could be said of me. I loved covering those games and somewhat hated them at the same time, because I just knew I would witness fan behavior that left a lot to be desired.

There is no doubt in my mind in order to accomplish anything of significance, whether in sports or in life, you have to bring your best effort. The big question is can you still have fun while you're doing it?

Everybody seems to have their game face on when something big is at stake. You look at the coaches on the sidelines and it appears somebody has just insulted their mother, their religion and their looks all at the same time. I often wonder what goes through their minds as they try to get the most out of their players.

I have been around hundreds of coaches through the years and watched a variety of styles and motivational tactics. I can honestly say I have never worked with anyone who is more intense than Aberdeen Central High School girls' basketball coach Dawn Seiler.

Dawn is an unbelievable coach and a good friend. We have shared many laughs through the years. However, you don't want to cross her path on game night.

I once told her, "Dawn, you would walk across your grandmother's grave if that's what it would take to win a game." Her response? "And my grandmother would want me to."

What's interesting is Dawn's daughter, Brooke, is a chip off the old block. The younger Seiler has now gotten into coaching, as well.

"She's more stubborn than I am," Seiler said of her daughter.

As a parent, did Dawn treat Brooke any differently than other players on the squad?

"You treat them as a team member. I don't think your expectations of them should be any different than any of the other athletes," she said of having children as players. "The difference is they have to go home with you."

And when Brooke went home, she actually provided her mom with a few coaching tips.

"She was really good at breaking down video and picking up things that I would miss," Dawn said. "We would talk about other teams and characteristics of players. She enjoyed doing that."

While there is no shortage of intensity and passion for excellence, the elder Seiler also understands the significant role sports plays in the lives of her players and it has a lot more meaning than simple X's and O's.

"We don't miss an opportunity to talk about life. We want this to be a learning experience," Seiler said. "We talk about athletics being an extension of the classroom. We can teach some real-life lessons. We get a chance to talk about a lot of issues that are going to come up during the course of their lifetime."

Seiler has dealt with a lot of parents and players during her 36 years of coaching. She said it is important parents feel they have a role in the program. Seiler said parents have a passion for the game and for their child, but sometimes can carry that too far.

She said the late Northern State men's basketball coaching great Don Meyer used to say, "Parents would rather have kids be all-state than win state."

While Seiler has won more girls' basketball games than any coach in South Dakota history, she clearly understands the significant role of athletics in today's society.

"Probably the buzz word in education right now is resilience," Seiler said. "We're not teaching our kids to be resilient."

For sure, coaches set the tone in practice, in the locker room and on the playing surface. Too much goofing around and it spells lack of focus and self-discipline. The last thing you want is a three-ring circus. While I can appreciate that intensity and passion, there are times when some practices can turn into a battlefield.

I've heard of one team where if players smile during practice, they are sent home for the day. I'm all about being serious when needed, but you also have to be able to enjoy a light-hearted moment and keep things in perspective. After all, it is still a ball game.

What parents and coaches need to keep in mind is even if you give 100 percent effort, at the end of the day, somebody is going to win and somebody is going to lose. You can make the argument if you haven't prepared for the battle, you have already lost. That is a proven point.

But the contests really don't come down to who hollers the loudest; who threatens the most. It's really not that simple. And there are multiple ways to motivate an athlete and they are proven to work. Whether a coach is a screamer like Bobby Knight or calm and composed like Mike Krzyzewski, there are multiple methods to experience success as a coach.

Former Milbank and Watertown wrestling coach Bob Hirsch won his share of matches during his hall of fame career. He found out hollering at athletes really doesn't help all that much.

"The first couple of years I was more of a screamer," Hirsch told me a while back. "Once the kids are out there, you can yell and scream all you want. Basically, the kids are going to wrestle their match or play their football." (American News, Feb. 19, 1999)

As parents, what's the best way to motivate our athletes? First, like coaches, we need to understand not all kids are wired the same and each responds differently. I know one thing for sure, unless coach is in your title, you certainly can't offer much in the way of advice on game day. Nor should you act like you know more than the individual coaching your son or daughter.

As I stated in a previous chapter, I have found that sometimes the people who holler the loudest during the games (most often the parents) are the ones who understand the rules and the concepts the least. Just because your son or daughter is a member of the team, even if he or she is the top player, does not make you an expert in the game.

Just like all successful teams have players who know their roles, all successful programs have individuals who know and fill those roles. Coaches coach, players play and parents need to be parents. If any of those roles get mixed up, you will end up with a dysfunctional program that will likely fall short of reaching its full potential.

And trust me, it's usually not the coaches who don't understand their role. I find it interesting that in South Dakota we have a coaching shortage when there seems to be so many qualified coaches sitting in the stands who think they know what's best for every player on the squad. There are several ramifications that come with that and none of them are good.

Not only do the parents try to undermine the coach (and sadly sometimes they get the job done), they also empower their sons or daughters to lose sight of their role on the team. I can't begin to tell you how many times I have been at a game where during a timeout I notice a player looking into the stands at mom or dad instead of paying attention to the coach. Those situations never turn out well for anybody involved.

So, what are parents to do if they don't approve of their child's extra-curricular experience? Unless it involves harassment or physical abuse, encourage your son or daughter to talk directly to the coach. Coaches don't want to deal with a parent who questions playing time or play calling. And if your athlete was to be totally honest, I doubt he or she would want that, either.

Besides, what are you teaching your children if you try to fight their battles for them? You can't do that in the working world, so there's no reason to attempt that in the sports world.

Let your sons or daughters earn their spot, support them AND the coach and you will likely have a positive and memorable experience.

14

INJURIES

Discover your gift, develop your gift and then give it away every day.
—Don Meyer

There's an old adage that says "nothing ventured, nothing gained." It probably applies to a lot of things in life, but it certainly is relevant in sports.

There is risk involved in everything and one of those risks in sport is injuries. It's something that can happen no matter how much precaution you take and it's something as a parent you can't do much about. Obviously, some injuries are worse than others, but all can either make or break an athlete.

It's August 2015 and Isaiah has had a full summer of tennis. We are down in Huron at the annual Pick Your Pie tournament. It's a fun little tennis event that is half social and half competitive. The tourney marks the official end of summer tennis. Little do we realize it will also mark the end of competitive sports for Isaiah for a long time.

Soon after that tourney in Huron, Isaiah begins complaining of a sore back. We think it might be out of place but are not overly concerned. He visits a chiropractor and continues to play basketball at open gym, although it is obvious he is not at full strength. A few weeks later, a red flag is raised.

Isaiah and I are out on the tennis courts ready to do battle against each other. He has improved through the years to the point where I have to be at the very top of my game to even make it competitive. I get off to a fast start and am feeling good about myself, oblivious to the fact he is not moving well. I soon realize we have a major problem on our hands when after the third game, he says, "I can't do this anymore."

A chiropractor suggests we visit a specialist who orders an MRI which turns into a diagnosis of a stress fracture of Isaiah's lower back. The remedy: no physical activity of any kind for 12 weeks. Nothing. No free weights, no lifting, not anything.

As Isaiah is fitted for a custom-made cumbersome back brace, we begin counting out the weeks to see how it will impact his sophomore season of basketball. Best case scenario is he misses the first four games of the season. Worst case scenario, it could be much more.

It is not easy watching a teenage boy who was physically active a month before being relegated to walking around on crutches and gimping around the house. While there are moments of frustration, Isaiah somehow manages to handle the situation much better than can be expected.

Again, as a parent, I probably am way more concerned about the return date to basketball than I should be.

Being a born-again Christian, I believe everything happens for a reason and God will use this for something positive. However, what transpires during the next 12 weeks still amazes me.

Isaiah has a keyboard in his room and with no real opportunity for physical activity, he begins to experiment and tries to learn a song. I watch as he limps out of his room, goes to the computer and studies music patterns, then goes back into his room to give it a try.

It is difficult and inspiring to watch at the same time.

Eventually, there is music coming from his room. It's short and there are occasional mistakes, but you can begin to recognize tunes.

By the time the 12 weeks are up, all of us, especially Isaiah, are ready to get rid of that brace. He gets it off on Christmas Eve day and says it's the best Christmas gift he could have asked for.

He is cleared to return to basketball practice and tries to play catchup the rest of the season. By the time he actually gets back into game shape, the season is nearly over. He still manages to play and is pretty much at full strength when tennis rolls around.

What my wife and I do not realize is a love of music has now been started in his life. He begins to play more and more often and soon he is playing the piano in church. We begin to have people coming up to us saying, "We didn't know Isaiah could play the piano." And our response is, "Neither did we."

Month after month, his love for music continues to grow. In the fall of 2017 he finds out we have an accordion in our basement that used to be my mom's. Soon, he is teaching himself how to play that.

He then has a discussion with Aberdeen Christian music instructor Andrew Granpdre. Isaiah asks if he can play the accordion on the school float in the Gypsy Day Parade, a homecoming event for Northern State University.

"Wait, what? You play the accordion?" Mr. Grandpre asks. "Yes," Isaiah responds. "Do you have an accordion?" Mr. Grandpre asks. "Yes," Isaiah says. "Well, OK then, let's give it a shot," the instructor replies.

I can honestly say, I have had many memorable moments as a parent, but watching my son go down Main Street on a float playing an accordion is something I never envisioned, nor will ever forget.

Soon, that love of music carries over to the guitar. Isaiah purchases a guitar for his birthday and basically teaches himself how to play. That leads to an expanded role in the school's praise team as well as at church.

Again, we have people coming up to us saying, "We didn't know Isaiah could play the guitar." Our response: "Neither did we."

I watched Isaiah learn and grow in both basketball and tennis, but to see him develop that musical talent was something I was not expecting. He was a two-time member of all-state chorus and eventually used that talent to become the leader of his school's praise team. And to think it all got kick-started because of a stress fracture in his lower back.

Nobody likes injuries and I'm convinced Isaiah didn't like his, either. However, it is a part of the game. Regardless of the activity and no matter how good of shape an athlete is in, there is always a risk involved.

I have had conversations with people who wonder out loud if playing sports is worth it, because of the inherent risk of injuries. While there is some merit to that logic, I grew up around the game and never really gave getting hurt a second thought.

Personally, I believe a person can get injured doing just about anything. If the logic is don't try something because you could get injured, you might end up missing out on a lot of things in life. It kind of goes back to that saying: "nothing ventured, nothing gained."

The fact of the matter is, you can't succeed unless you try. There are enough people walking around looking for excuses not to be physically active. We certainly don't need to give them another reason.

Now, I am all about player safety and I think there are ways to prevent injuries. In fact, with all of the advances in stretching, diet, equipment and techniques, today's athletes should be more prepared than ever to combat the risks of competing in sports.

That is why I am big proponent of multi-sport athletes. I am not a fan of sports specialization. I know it happens and its frequency is on the rise.

I also understand this is fast becoming a way of life in big schools. The larger the school, the more athletes feel the need to spend all of their time and effort in a single sport.

That leads to problems on multiple fronts. For starters, there have been studies done that have shown single sport athletes are much more likely to get injured because of non-stop repetitive motion. In fact, just the slight difference between throwing a football and throwing a baseball can make a huge difference.

Second, it leads to a major issue during the "offseason," a time when an athlete needs a break from his or her sport. We have now reached the point where some high school athletes never do take time off from their sport. It used to be when I was growing up, you would compete in football in the fall, basketball in the winter, track in the spring and baseball in the summer. Plus fit in a time for family vacation. Rare is that athlete today.

Now, athletes are often forced to pick a sport (or two) and focus their entire attention on that. Basketball camps and leagues pretty much run year around. Soccer is much the same way. In fact, coaches are starting to compete against each other when it comes to finding time to share athletes who do play multiple sports.

I know some coaches who feel the need to have year around programs, because the school down the road is doing it and they don't want to fall behind.

However, I have yet to meet a college coach who wants a recruit to solely participate in one sport in high school. So, who is giving that advice to high school athletes? While some of their coaches do play a role in this, I think the majority of this thinking can be traced right back to parents.

At the very least, you could make the argument coaches feel pressured to win as many games as possible so they want to get to as many camps and leagues as possible and that pressure to succeed and win a championship originates with parents and administration.

Could my son have been a better basketball player or tennis player had he concentrated on just one sport and spent his entire life refining those skills? Maybe, but at what cost?

Instead, he played in some off-season tournaments and leagues. He seldom went weeks without competing in something. However, he also got involved in other things. He went on mission trips and attended camp with the church's youth group. He gave tennis lessons to help the next generation of players. In short, he took time to be a teenage kid, and I wouldn't have wanted it any other way.

I'm all about maximizing potential, but I think we are doing kids a disservice when we tell them to put all of their eggs into one basket and give up everything else. I know of an individual who was a stellar multi-sport athlete as a youth. He decided to concentrate on a single sport and I'm not sure it proved to be a sound decision in the end.

In my opinion the appeal of sports specialization is the belief that if you concentrate on just one thing, it will lead to more success in that particular event, which isn't always the case.

Hall of fame athlete, coach and athletic director Jim Haar has witnessed that trend. He shared his thoughts on how things have changed through the years.

"I can remember football, basketball, track, baseball; football, basketball, track, baseball. Now it's football, football, football or basketball, basketball, basketball. I don't know, they all seem to think, is it a dream that they want to go to the big-time college or a dream that they'll some time become a professional athlete? I'm not sure what it is, but that's probably the thing that bothers me the most and that is that kids do not get involved in multiple sports at their high school careers." (Legends Sports Show, Oct. 18, 2018).

As mentioned in a previous chapter, colleges are now looking at potential recruits as early as middle school. Parents are drinking the Kool-Aid, transporting kids as young as fifth and sixth grade all across the country looking for the best competition in hopes of developing their son or daughter as the next star player. Families are becoming more and more fragmented as they rush their children from one event to another. Again, there is no guarantee any of this extra playing time will be beneficial, but there is no arguing there is a huge cost to pay by trying it.

Is it any wonder why coaches are burned out after just a few years or there is a lack of officials because they are getting berated at elementary school games? This is what sports have evolved into and it's a sad commentary on what we have become as a society.

Look, I am very competitive by nature and I always wanted my kids to be as successful as possible. I am ashamed to admit their shortcomings sometimes bothered me worse than them. However, I have also been able to take a step back and see things for what they are. I have been around sports my entire life, and it appears they have started to consume most of us.

I can honestly tell you I enjoyed watching my son perform with the school's praise and worship team as much as I liked watching him play basketball or tennis. And that's saying something for a sports junkie like me.

Looking back at the fall of 2015, it was a bit like Charles Dickens Tale of Two Cities only in reverse. It was the worst of times that turned into the best of times. It's true nobody like injuries, but sometimes they are unavoidable, and in some instances, they really can be a blessing in disguise.

15

RELEVANCE

I never once mentioned to my team that we've got to win a game.
I always talked about preparing to win.
—Jim Leyland

We all want to be successful, whatever your definition of success may be.

For some it's all about winning. For others, it's primarily about statistics. For others it might be effort or improvement. No matter what your measurement of success might be, we all want it and we all want it on a consistent basis.

The problem is we all make mistakes and sometimes those mistakes are magnified. Personally, I need to be reminded from time to time that we all fail. I know I am guilty of thinking high school players should play as well as college players, college players as well as professionals. Yet, even pro athletes exhibit a lack of judgment and don't make every play, even the one that may seem routine.

That is where my wife Lauretta, comes in. She has a way of keeping things in perspective. On more than one occasion she helped to calm me down when Isaiah was having a tough shooting night. While I wondered out loud how he could miss an easy shot, it was Lauretta who would say, "Dave, relax. It's not like he's trying to miss them."

I'm not sure that made me feel any better, because I knew she was correct and I was wrong, and Isaiah's shooting percentage still wasn't any better because of it.

Maybe it's the competitor in me or maybe it's because I knew the potential my son possessed, but when he had an off-shooting night, I had a tough time dealing with it. That's when I was reminded about what was really important in life.

Aberdeen Christian is playing Faulkton. Christian is coming off its first loss of the season and is playing at home against a dangerous Faulkton team which struggled early in the year. On paper, it is a winnable game, especially considering Faulkton is without one of its top players for the contest due to illness.

The night is a study in frustration. Shots aren't falling, defensive stops aren't coming and it looks like the Trojans might just be recalling Isaiah's last-second shot on their home court the year before. I'm sure the smoke is probably billowing out of my ears as Faulkton closes in on a solid road win.

I am starting to lament how Isaiah could have played better and how the team is on its way to back-to-back losses after eight straight victories when all of the sudden I spot Faulkton Athletic Director Craig Cassens out of the corner of my eye. A very guilty feeling instantly comes over me.

Craig's son, Christopher, had been killed in a car accident about 16 months before. He was nearly the same age as Isaiah. I cannot begin to imagine the heartache the family has gone through. I lower my head, completely ashamed of my thoughts about tonight's ball game. I know the Cassens would do anything to have their son back and here am I having a meltdown over something as insignificant as a basketball game. I immediately understand how blessed I am that I can watch my son play, regardless of the outcome of the contest.

There are some people that believe sports are nothing more than entertainment. I don't necessarily agree with that notion, but I do think we swing the pendulum too far the other direction and make games out to be much more than they should be. At the very least, they should be a stress release, not a stress builder. However, there we are on a weekly basis, front row center, cheering on the players, screaming at the officials and second-guessing the coaches. Not sure that sounds like a stress-free situation to me.

I do know this much, when you live in South Dakota, you definitely need a diversion to make it through the hard winter months. Days become long, nights even longer and it can seem like there is no end to the brutal elements in sight. It's nice to have games to attend and teams to follow to help keep our mind off the sub-zero temperatures and lack of sunshine.

I honestly don't know what I would do if I didn't attend games during the winter months. I'm sure the winters would seem even longer than they are.

I do believe, however, there is a major difference between watching other people's kids and watching your own. While we as parents cannot alter the results whether we have a child participating or not, we feel much more invested when our offspring are playing. We also feel justified in our actions no matter how silly or childish they appear to others around us.

I once knew a guy who was very pleasant to be around before his sons played high school athletics. During that four-year span when he had sons on the squad, he became a completely different person. Gone was the happy-go-lucky guy, replaced with some cynical over-bearing parent who always thought his sons were better than they actually were. As soon as they graduated, he went right back to the same jolly man that I knew years before. I thought to myself, I don't want to become one of "those parents."

I recently ran into a man who used to have children in athletics. I told him about the book I was working on. He said something to me that I think is pretty spot on, even if he was half-joking. "It's funny. Now that our kids are done playing, I've noticed the coaching has gotten much better," he said, "and now that our kids are done playing, I've noticed that the officiating has gotten much better."

You would think knowing there is a trap lying before you, a person would be cognizant of avoiding that pitfall. I am here to tell you, it is not that easy. Even after being reminded on numerous occasions high school athletics are just a game and not a matter of life and death, I still managed to fall prey to the lure of becoming too involved.

(It is the danger that goes along with being the parent trapped within).

It's a beautiful Friday afternoon in Rapid City. Sioux Park is a hub of activity. There is action on all 12 tennis courts. Right beside the facility a track and field meet is taking place featuring dozens of athletes. I should be content that I am out of the office and watching tennis on a weekday afternoon.

Instead, it is another one of those days where I don't think Isaiah is playing up to expectations (my expectations). He continues to make one unforced error after another. Before I realize it, the words pour out of my mouth. "That's pathetic. How many balls can you possibly hit into the net?" I blurt out.

I immediately look around to see if anybody hears me. I can't believe that I am turning into one of "those parents."

Of course, it takes a milli-second for God to offer a fresh perspective on the situation. If I am not already feeling bad enough, I glance over to the track meet directly beside me. There I see a group of Special Olympics athletes heading back to their bus, broad smiles on their faces, happy to be out competing.

They are clearly enjoying life to the fullest and here am I, standing behind a baseline fence not enjoying the moment at all. Another life-lesson learned through athletics, and not just by the athlete.

I'm sure I am not alone in my emotions when it comes to watching children compete in extra-curricular activities. In fact, I know that I am not.

There is a fine line between putting up with average and demanding perfection. Neither of which is acceptable. We all want our children to perform up their potential and when they don't (which is going to happen routinely), we have to know how to deal with that. What so many of us fail to understand is how much pressure is on these kids in the first place.

When I recall my teenage years, I remember all of the stress I was under. I wouldn't go back to that time in my life for anything. While I certainly had a lot of enjoyable moments, I also recall all of the uncertainties (where I was going to college, who I would marry, what I would do for a profession, the list goes on and on). Add in all the pressure of meeting others' expectations on an athletic field and it's easy to see why the game isn't fun at all for some athletes, even those who experience a lot of success.

There was a standout athlete I interviewed once who was preparing for her final state track and field meet. She had qualified in numerous events and had the top time and distance in many of them. In short, she was an elite performer who was expected to win every time she competed.

As the conversation unfolded, I asked her what her future plans were. She told me she was going to attend a certain university. It happened to be that the school was NCAA Division I and featured a very competitive track and field program. "Oh, that's nice. They have a solid track and field program. You'll fit right in," I said. "Oh, I'm not running track in college," she said. "I hate it. I can't wait until I'm finished."

Wait. What? I had a hard time understanding how somebody could be so successful in an activity and find so little enjoyment in it. I am not sure exactly what her situation entailed, but somewhere along the line, I have a hunch a parent forced her to participate or perhaps put too much pressure on her to excel. Whatever the case, I hung the up the phone feeling a tinge of sadness for her. She had a true gift that was not going to be used to its fullest extent.

It's not that things are supposed to be easy in life. In fact, just the opposite. If you want to obtain something of value, it should never come easy. However, it doesn't matter what extra-curricular activity your child is involved in, at the very foundation it has to be fun and enjoyable. It will be very difficult to reach full potential and true success without that.

For sure there will be highs and lows and plenty of hardships and heartaches along the way, just like life itself. But I have found through experience the pleasure has to outweigh the pain otherwise it doesn't work. The athlete will be miserable, the chemistry will be chaotic and the results will lack fulfillment.

Of course, it's always more fun to win than lose, but nobody wins all of the time.

It's interesting, because I have interviewed many of the winningest coaches in South Dakota history. When I ask them about the most memorable seasons they have had, a lot of them will not mention a state championship season. In fact, many of them will point to a team that had marginal talent and expectations were low. The coach will then go on to explain how that team reached its full potential, won more games than it lost and perhaps even made it to a state tournament.

Ask any coach and he or she will tell you it takes talent to win state titles. However, true success cannot be measured simply in terms of championships or even wins and losses.

While fans and parents might remember those title teams or even season records, the ones who know the most about those squads will tell you there is a lot more to athletics than what occurs on game day.

16

DOWN THE STRETCH

What you are as a person is far more important
than what you are as a basketball player.
—*John Wooden*

No matter how often we think we have things all figured out, high school athletics can turn our thoughts upside down with their sheer unpredictability. We always hear the adage: on any given night anybody can beat anybody. That's really a wonderful thing, because it gives underdogs hope and favorites cause to guard against complacency. Of course, it can drive coaches and fans nuts.

As a parent, watching events unfold with no degree of certainty can be a major source of stress. Throw in the end of a career for a high school senior and the stakes become much higher.

It is during that time where you just have to appreciate the journey, knowing the road will soon come to an end. And that road can be full of twists and turns, peaks and valleys with little warning of what's coming next.

This is all set up to be a very fun weekend. We are in Watertown playing Great Plains Lutheran. Isaiah will have more family at this game than any other of his athletic events during his career.

Not only is the normal crew of relatives in the building, his grandma is sitting courtside alongside one of his aunts. There is also a delegation of family that has made the trek over from Minnesota. In all, there are 13 total family members at the game.

As I sit in the stands, I think this could be a huge day. Isaiah is due for a big game and the team needs to regain its early-season form.

The contest soon becomes memorable for all the wrong reasons. Aberdeen Christian leads most of the way, but has a hard time shaking the Panthers who are geared up because it is Parents Day with plenty of fanfare. In addition to guided tours of the school, many players (some from as far away as Alabama and Utah) have their own family members in attendance because of the festivities.

Isaiah has another tough shooting game, but his woes are nothing compared to mine. Maybe it's because I want him to play well so badly because his relatives are present or maybe it's because I know what he is capable of, but on this day, it is one of the rare times I lose it.

After a series of missed shots, I suddenly blurt out, "Man, what is going on? We've got to get his eyes checked!"

As soon as the words escape my mouth, I begin to look around to see who might have heard me. Man, don't tell me I'm becoming one of "those parents."

Isaiah makes just 1 of 3 free throws down the stretch, but to be fair, one was half way down and popped out. The big thing is, the team won and we need it because we are fighting for seeding in one of the best regions in the state.

Up next in two nights is a game against Britton-Hecla on the road.

"We'll have to play a lot better to win that game than we did tonight," says a fellow parent. There is no arguing from me.

Just 48 hours later we pull into Britton. This will be a battle like none other. The Braves are playing well and are breathing down Aberdeen Christian's neck in the seed-point chase.

As I watch the girls' game play out, I realize we are badly outnumbered in fan count. I decide this will be it. I am going to bring it tonight. No more passiveness, no more wondering who is watching me. I am going to be vocal. Positive, but vocal.

While I feel extremely out of character, I let my voice be heard all game. And what a game it is. Christian leads the whole way, but as expected the Braves mount a huge fourth-quarter comeback.

It is tight and the tension is high. I holler encouragement to the players. The Braves turn up the heat with full-court pressure and I know the game will likely come down to a free-throw shooting contest at the end.

The Knights hold up their end of the bargain at the line, but the Braves, namely Kyler Meyer, are making three-pointers like crazy, trading three points for two. They end up fouling Isaiah multiple times and he finally makes foul shots like he is capable of. He nails 5 of 6 in the final two minutes and we hold on for the win.

I am spent, physically and emotionally, and I never even played. I know there could be a rematch down the road in the region, but for now, I am ecstatic. This was a quality win on the road and my son played a key role. This is a night I will remember for a long time.

Knowing the end of a season is coming should help a person prepare for it, but it's much different when you have a vested interest. Game days feel much different around the house. Inwardly, you start counting down the number of potential games remaining.

I am sure all parents envision their son or daughter making a last-second shot or having a huge scoring game. It's only natural they do. There are some people that believe unless you can picture something like that occurring it likely won't take place. I'm here to tell you there is a high likelihood even if you dream about it, chances are it might still not take place.

That is where the real lessons happen. As a parent, you should be supportive no matter what the outcome and learn to appreciate your athletes for who they are and what they bring to the game. Remember, you are learning life-lessons through athletics just like your son or daughter.

The snow is flying and the conditions are deteriorating as we pull into Bowdle on a Thursday night in February. Aberdeen Christian is playing Eureka-Bowdle and the snow outside turns into rain inside as the Knights open the game by raining down three-pointers from the opening whistle.

Christian explodes out to a 30-4 lead in the opening quarter. Isaiah scores 10 of the quickest points of his life and I think to myself, this could be the night. He could go off for 25-30 points easily.

However, as the game plays out, it suddenly occurs to me my son is not that type of player. Instead of jacking up shots in attempt to get a career high, he dishes off to open teammates to make sure they are involved. He is not even close to being the leading scorer by the end of the game and I am totally fine with that. Basketball is a team game and if the Knights are going to make any noise in the post-season they will have to do it as a team.

When you know something is inevitable it tends to be a bit easier to deal with. However, when that something is the end of a senior's high school basketball career, I'm not convinced that applies. That ending could be prolonged or it could be abrupt, but like time itself, you can't stop it from coming. That's where enjoying the journey really comes in.

It's about 10 minutes before game-time on a Friday night at the Aberdeen Civic Arena. Aberdeen Christian is hosting Northwestern in its final regular-season home game.

I am standing near center court getting ready to announce the starting lineups like I have for every home game all season. A mother of another player walks by and asks, "Are you sad? This is your son's final home game."

I smile and say, "No. I know that this is special, but I don't want him to stay in high school forever."

I understand while tonight's game is important, the next game will be even more crucial because it will take place in the Region 1B tournament. It will be win and advance or lose and go home.

As expected, that region foe turns out to be Britton-Hecla. The contest takes place in Clark and I know this will be another knock-down, drag-out battle just like the prior meeting.

While the contest takes place on a neutral floor, there are plenty of fans there from both sides and the atmosphere is electric. I try to mentally prepare for the worst, hope for the best and decide I am going to leave nothing left in the tank.

While I don't realize it at the time, my cheering, while positive, is either excessive or totally out of character, because at one stage I look over at my sister-in-law, Kathy, and she gives me the "settle down" signal.

Here's my barometer that there really is no tomorrow: Lauretta accidentally bumps somebody while cheering during the contest. That never happens.

The contest is just what I envisioned it would be, tight, physical, intense, and full of emotion. This is going to go down to the wire just like the first meeting.

The Knights again lead most of the way, only this time Britton-Hecla is able to take the lead midway through the fourth quarter. Christian battles back and has a chance to win the game in the closing seconds, but the Knights come up empty and the game goes to overtime.

As a member of the media, I actually love close games. As a parent of a player on the floor with the season on the line, I am not quite as fond of them.

In a cruel twist of fate that sports sometimes provide, Britton-Hecla appears to have the game won late in overtime, only to have the Knights come back with a chance to pull out an improbably victory that falls one point short. The game ends in bizarre fashion as Isaiah steals an in-bounds pass in the backcourt and Christian misses two off-balance attempts (one by Isaiah) before the final horn sounds.

I am officially numb. All of the years of going to YMCA games, camps, open gyms and contests through the years has come to an end. A bitter end. I have been a part of these kinds of games for nearly four decades, but never as a parent of a player whose basketball career has just come to an end.

Being a man of my word, there are no excuses, no regrets. That is something I've always preached and I am not going to change now. I walk back to the locker room area to find the players, but they have already boarded the van and are ready to head home.

I congratulate Britton-Hecla coach Travis Santistevan and wish him and the Braves well in their upcoming semifinal game.

I knew Christian's season was in jeopardy of ending at any time in the post season, just like anybody else. I was just hoping tonight would not be that time.

Like I had so many times before, I videotape the final sequence of the contest in case something special happens. I know I have my son's final moments caught on tape, but I cannot bring myself to watch it right now. That will have to wait for another day.

Upon returning home, I try not to say the wrong thing to Isaiah. Naturally, he is disappointed to say the least and rightfully so, because if he isn't, that means he has not invested much. We both know the contest could have easily gone the other way, but again, no excuses are made and there will be more time for reflection in the next few days.

Two nights later Britton-Hecla's season comes to an end in a loss in the region semifinals. Such is the nature of sports.

I often talk with my co-workers about which is the most difficult way to have a season end: with a lopsided loss in which you didn't play up to your potential or with a heart-breaking setback in which the outcome was in doubt until the closing seconds? Arguments can be made for both and I'm not sure there is a clear-cut choice. And make no mistake, either way hurts.

In talking with a few coaches of multiple sports, they prefer to go down swinging, even if it means a gut-wrenching last-second defeat. Personally, I think you tend to second-guess yourself in those close games, because you always think of a play or two that could have gone the other way. Lopsided losses are easier to deal with if the opponent is far more superior, but much tougher if your team did not play up to its potential.

No matter what, though, it is totally unfair to judge a team based solely on its final game. By that standard, most would be labeled failures because very few teams are fortunate enough to win their last contest.

17

RATIONALE

When you win, say nothing.
When you lose, say less.
—Paul Brown

Regardless of the location or the activity, one thing is certain in sports: people love their favorite players and teams. Their loyalty is unwavering and can sometimes push people over the edge in their support.

It's really interesting, because in reality, whether a certain team wins or loses seldom has any direct impact on the majority of individuals in this world. However, don't try telling that to a Red Sox fan following a win over the Yankees or a Duke fan after a victory over North Carolina. People live vicariously through their favorite team.

There's nothing wrong with supporting a specific team or a player. It's when it becomes an obsession that problems arise. Of course, when it involves parents of players on high school teams, it often becomes emotional warfare.

Unfortunately, we have reached a time in our society where following a loss, coaches, parents and fans have to come up with an explanation. It is no longer good enough to say, congratulations, we got beat by a better team tonight. Oh no, there has be some sort of explanation beyond that to justify what transpired.

Stop me if you have heard these comments before: "it's tough to play five on seven; they could have called holding on them every play; those guys got so lucky; it just wasn't our night; half our girls were sick; you can never win playing in that cracker box of a gym; those refs were out to get us tonight; those boys are just so rough; they are a much bigger school than we are; just wait until next time."

While some of those comments may even have a hint of accuracy to them, they certainly shouldn't be substituted for things like "nice job, good game, best of luck in the future."

I understand it's not fun to come up on the short end and sometimes it hurts even more when so much is at stake, but it still doesn't justify the type of behavior that has become more and more prevalent today.

It's the championship round of the State B Wrestling tournament and the atmosphere is electric. The finest wrestlers in South Dakota are one step away from coveted state titles.

Being a member of the media, I am as close to the mat as you can get. Not only can I get a great view of the action, I have immediate access to the competitors as soon as the matches are finished.

As the match I am covering is nearing an end, I have no idea I am about to become involved in one of the most memorable situations of my professional career.

Following the match, I walk over to the winner and begin an interview. Much to my surprise, in the middle of a response, a woman comes over and starts to berate the state's newest champion. Her language is hostile and includes a variety of name-calling.

I am totally confused, as is the individual I am interviewing. As the woman concludes and walks away, I ask the wrestler if he knows who that is. He says no. As I glance over, I see the opponent's last name on the back of her sweatshirt and soon realize it is the runner-up's mom.

I have never had an exchange with a fan before, but I am not going to let this one go. I walk over and soon the mom and I have our own little debate.

"You have no right to come over and say the things that you did," I begin.

"Did you see what he did?" asks the mom, complaining about how the opponent's style hurt her son's chances of winning the title.

"It doesn't matter. He didn't commit a crime or anything," I explain. "I want you to know that you are way out of line."

The conversation continues for a short while longer, with neither one of us conceding an inch.

As I walk away, my blood is pumping and it feels a bit like I have just competed in a state championship match.

"That was bizarre," says a fellow media member who has just witnessed the whole thing.

No truer words have ever been spoken.

What's interesting about the encounter is the mother was not complaining her son was getting roughed up. In fact, she was upset because she felt her son's opponent was employing a style that was ducking her son. Regardless of her logic, it just shows how emboldened parents have become in support of their children.

I really wish I could say that was the only time I have witnessed that type of behavior. Unfortunately, it is not.

The consolation round game of the state girls' basketball tournament has just finished and I am interviewing the winning coach as usual.

During one of my questions, I am startled and stunned to find a woman has joined in on the conversation. She proceeds to let the coach have an earful about his coaching demeanor and style on the sidelines. Apparently, she is upset about him running up the score or something, and whatever it is, she is not getting cheated in letting her opinion be known.

The coach turns about four shades of red, does not offer a rebuttal and then tries to get back to answering my questions. I am not even sure what to ask after that. All I know is the coach regains his composure quickly enough to provide comments for the game story I will write.

For whatever reason, call it pride, arrogance, unwillingness to accept defeat, whatever, people not only do not like to lose, they feel they have been somehow cheated if they do come up on the short end.

While it doesn't always have to include parents, I believe the most extreme cases do. How else could you even begin to explain that type of irrational behavior?

Now, I'm not saying people have to cave in and say the opposing foe has the best team. In fact, sometimes the best team doesn't always win. But you always need to display good sportsmanship and never give your athlete a reason to complain. When people focus on excuses, they don't focus on execution.

An opponent might have outplayed you and in fact they may be better than you and that's OK. If that's the case, live with it and move on. However, I have also seen this used as justification for a team's shortcomings.

Year after year, all I ever hear from coaches and fans is, our region is so tough, we have the best teams in the state in our region. And the thing is, fans from all across the state feel the same way. And guess what? They can't all have the toughest region. Very seldom do I ever hear anybody say, our region is so weak.

The fact of the matter is, to be the best you have to beat the best. Winning state championships do not come easy and there is some luck involved. I believe everybody at every level has to catch a break to win anything of significance. It may not come in the title contest, but at some spot along the playoff run something out of the ordinary has to go your way (a banked in shot, a fumble that bounces the right way, etc.). Those are things you really cannot control.

The problem is some parents think they can control those things. Some wait until the results are finished and then voice their disapproval to their own coach, the opposing coach, their own players or opposing players. Others make their opinions heard before the contests transpire. And then there are those parents who try to coach while a game is in progress.

I know of one parent who actually got up out of the stands, walked down to the sidelines and tried to tell a coach what play to run while a game was going on. I had another media member tell me of an incident he witnessed where the parents walked across the middle of a football field while a play was in progress to go over and chew out the coach for hollering at their son. Incredible.

I am sure this type of behavior takes place in other extra-curricular activities as well, such as debating who gets the lead role in the school drama or who makes first chair in band, but there is something about sports in particular that gets people going. And whatever the rationale seems to be, I do believe at the very core of the issue are parents who always want a little more for their son or daughter.

"It can be a major headache," said former Webster volleyball coach Cindy Nelson in a project I did on coaching. "Some of my darkest moments in coaching have been dealing with parents." (American News, Feb. 19, 1999)

Questionable parental behavior is something that's been around forever, but it has gotten worse. Can those thought processes be changed? Is there too much emphasis placed on winning? Certainly, there is too much self-centered thinking at the center of it all.

It's not that all sports parents are bad. Far, far from it. It's just when games start, it's hard for parents to remain objective. I know that from first-hand experience.

(It's hard to escape being the parent trapped within).

Many parents volunteer as concession workers, ticket takers, announcers, etc. While their intentions may be good and schools need workers to put on events, I have seen problems arise when parents are put in positions of authority at games.

I have witnessed a parent making a questionable call on match point as a line judge in a volleyball match. I have seen a parent lose his composure as a member of the chain gang and throw his down-marker at an opposing player. I have seen a parent get so enthusiastic behind the microphone about his son's team it caused an opposing fan to come over and tell him to tone down the rhetoric. Don't even get me started about parents running the score clock of tight games.

These individuals are good people. They are law-abiding citizens who are respected members of their communities. It's just when their sons or daughters are involved, things can happen in the heat of the moment. Unfortunately, those things tend to be remembered for a long time.

Look, parents need to be active in their children's lives. We have all witnessed the ugly consequences when they are not. They just need to remain positive, understanding and supportive as everybody learns life-lessons through the peaks and valleys of athletics.

18
PARENTAL GUIDANCE

If you are going to make every game a matter of life or death,
you are going to have lots of problems.
For one thing, you'll be dead a lot.
—Dean Smith

The majority of kids get their start in athletics from their parents. From playing catch in the backyard to shooting hoops in the driveway or in our case, tagging along to the tennis courts, kids often get their first exposure to some sort of sporting activity from mom or dad.

There is absolutely nothing wrong with that. In fact, it is admirable that parents want to spend time with their kids and show them how to learn the basics of a game. Some parents will go on to coach their children's little league teams.

Perhaps that's why it is so hard for parents to take a step back when their kids get older. They are used to coaching their children and often times feel they know what is best for them more so than their son's or daughter's current coach. That can lead to major problems.

Sometimes that parental involvement has nothing to do with coaching, but more with looking out for their child's best interest. It has been my experience that whether justified or not, whenever a parent becomes an active part of a contest, bad things are bound to happen.

It's the last weekend of July and as usual I am filling my position as director of the Hub City Open Tennis Tournament. Each year the tourney presents various sorts of challenges, from people not being on time to play their matches to others taking exception to the pre-tourney draws. Seldom does the event run perfectly smooth from start to finish. It will not happen this year, either.

I always try to participate in the event in addition to running it. On this particular occasion Lauretta and I are on the court playing a mixed doubles match when it happens. This year's issue is developing on the court directly south of ours and lo and behold it involves a parent.

The match features two out of town players, one an adult and the other a high school player. However, the real issue happens to be the mom sitting in the stands who thinks that her daughter is being cheated on line calls.

As I look over, the two players are arguing at midcourt. I put down my racquet and walk over to try and settle the issue. I listen to both sides before saying, "Ladies, this is not the U.S. Open. This is recreational tennis. Do you think you can get through this?"

The two gals, though visibly upset with each other, decide to give it a shot. I call over a co-worker to monitor the rest of the match and they finish up without any more incidents.

The real kicker to the story is that before the tournament starts, one of the gals is looking for a doubles partner in the tourney. I just so happen to pair them up a couple of days before the event starts. Now, the two players who were at each other's throats just a few minutes earlier are supposed to be teammates on the same side of the net for a doubles match. Talk about awkward.

I ask the two gals if they will still consider playing with each other and much to my surprise they say yes. In a crazy twist of irony, those two go on to win the championship of their doubles division. You just can't make this stuff up.

Through the years I've heard of parents who have given their son or daughter subliminal signals on whether balls were in or out. I've seen parents get involved when players can't recall the score. When that occurs, the results are usually nothing but bad.

That's why whenever I watched one of Isaiah's matches, I always tried to stay out of it. Even if I knew I was right (and sometimes I wasn't sure myself), I would never try to tell the players what the score should be if they couldn't remember. There were actually a couple of times when I knew my son's opponent was clearly wrong, but the last thing I wanted to do was become a part of the match from the sideline. I knew that was going to be a no-win situation. I know how frustrated I would have felt had another parent got involved in one of Isaiah's matches. Parents need to support and be there for their children. They are not coaches and they are not officials.

I can guarantee you, during a match, about the last thing Isaiah wanted from me was advice on things he was doing wrong. He certainly wouldn't tolerate me weighing in on scores or line calls, nor should he.

It's interesting, because during my years as a sports writer I witnessed numerous opportunities where mistakes were made during basketball games. I saw missed baskets counted as good, three-pointers counted as two-pointers, points failed to be put on the scoreboard, etc. I also knew my position. I was a member of the media, not the official scorekeeper.

If those in charge asked me for a score check, I would give it to them. If not, I basically kept my mouth shut. (Besides, I am also human and there were times I made mistakes as well).

One of the most memorable miscues took place in a very tight girls' basketball contest.

A team is credited with making a free throw that clearly misses. While most of the people in the gym don't catch it, a student manager and I both notice the error. Again, we are not the official scorer and the point gets put on the scoreboard. Unfortunately, the contest goes into overtime and the team that benefits from the error ends up winning.

Following the contest during my post-game interview, I tell the coach, "You know, you never should have won that game tonight." He says, "I know. We didn't play very well."

I respond, "No, I mean you never should have won that game. They gave you an extra point."

I then explain how his team benefitted from a missed free throw that was counted as good.

I wish I could say that was the only example of that kind of human error I witnessed in person, but it wasn't even the most memorable one I was involved in.

I am sitting courtside for a boys' district basketball championship. The game has been tight the whole way and it appears the outcome will be decided in the closing seconds.

Late in regulation, a player drives to the hoop and as a collision takes place in the lane he throws the ball toward the basket. The official closest to the play is concentrating on whether to make a block or charge call and doesn't watch the ball, which does not go in the basket.

The official calls a block and then asks his partner whether the ball went in or not. The official mistakenly says yes and the team is credited with two points. I am dumbfounded.

I look around and say out loud, "That ball didn't go in, did it? I'm sure it didn't go in."

Again, I am a member of the media, and nobody else, including the coach of the team who just had a major call go against his squad, is arguing. Hmm. Maybe I missed it, but I'm pretty sure that ball didn't go in.

The contest goes to overtime and of course, the team which benefitted from the generous call ends up winning.

Two days later, I get a call at work from an irate person connected to the losing team. After somebody watches film of the game, my suspicions are confirmed: that ball did not go in the basket. The individual on the phone thinks it was my place to go over and tell the official scorer they should not have counted the basket.

For starters, I was not 100 percent sure I was correct. Second, I inform the caller that is not my job. The coach should have called the officials over and told them about the call. It was his team that had something at stake, not me.

Looking back on that situation, I have no idea what position the caller held, but I think it was probably a parent.

In both of the aforementioned instances I questioned out loud about the accuracy of what took place. However, there have also been other times where I thought I was right only to find out I was the one in error.

I understand we all make mistakes. Human errors, whether by an umpire or a scorekeeper or line judge are just a part of the game and very seldom do they actually determine the outcome of a game. Even in the previous examples of added points, there were still plays that could have been made to switch the outcome the other way.

Again, as a parent this is a teachable moment. Let your athlete know sometimes calls go their way and sometimes they do not. It's how you handle those situations that matter most. Don't empower them to think others are out to get them. If you allow that sort of thinking, they will soon start doubting every call, begin making excuses for every setback, and never reach their full potential as an athlete, let alone as a person. Parents can either be part of the problem or part of the solution.

As mentioned previously, tennis is one of those sports where each of the players is responsible for making their own calls. Mistakes can happen. I get it. But I always told Isaiah, if somebody is calling lines pretty tight, hit a better shot. Make sure the ball is well inside the line so there is no doubt whether it is in or not. Again, you can make excuses or you can make a play.

Coaches, you can defuse a lot of these problems as well. Trust me, officials are not out to get you. If you are constantly complaining about calls, players and fans will follow suit. Stick up for your players, but also provide an example of how to handle adversity when it comes. These teenagers will soon be adults and be confronted with situations that aren't necessarily fair. While it may be difficult during the heat of the battle, remember it's not all about winning or losing. It's about teaching lessons that those you have been entrusted to mentor will be able to use throughout their lifetimes.

19

RECIPE FOR SUCCESS

Our emphasis is on execution, not winning.
—Pat Summitt

As society has evolved, so has the world of sports and the elements surrounding them. Athletes have gotten bigger, stronger and faster as equipment, training and nutrition has improved. However, the one thing that has remained a constant through the years is the desire to be successful.

It's interesting to see various coaches employ different strategies, all with the same goal in mind. Everybody is always looking for an edge, trying to find a better way.

Yet, it has been my experience some of the winningest coaches I have covered through the years still like to keep things relatively simple. Not that they don't try new concepts, but at the end of the day, they believe doing the little things will add up to something big.

Todd Thorson has built a running dynasty at Ipswich High School. Year in and year out the Tigers field some of the most competitive cross country and track and field squads in the state. The Ipswich girls won seven straight Class B state cross-country championships and five consecutive Class B state track and field titles often in record-setting fashion.

Back in 2013, during the Tigers' dominant run, Thorson talked about his team as it prepared to break its own scoring record at the state track meet from the season before. While the Tigers had the chance to place high in many individual events, that was not at the forefront of Thorson's thoughts.

"We don't worry about place," Thorson said at the time. "Winning events has never been a high priority. I think you set kids up for failure when you talk strictly about winning."

Boom!

That goes against the winning at all cost philosophy so prevalent in our society today. If our definition of success is winning, most of our athletes are going to fail. That simply cannot be the standard and parents need to understand that.

Ipswich has become the gold standard behind Thorson who preaches attitude, effort and improvement.

"We're a team and it's all about personal improvement. It shouldn't be about beating this kid or that kid," Thorson said as he prepared for that state meet in 2013. "The goal is still the same. Get better every day and you're a winner." (American News, May 8, 2013)

A few weeks later the Tigers went out and obliterated the field, winning another state championship with a then-record 116 points. The second-place squad finished with 37 ½ points.

Of course, it takes a combination of talent, work ethic and a few breaks to accomplish something truly special in athletics. Those things were on display for the Warner volleyball team during its record-breaking season in 2012.

The Monarchs set a national record by not dropping a single set on the way to winning the State B championship. Warner won 34 straight matches and a whopping 90 consecutive sets. That squad was named the MaxPreps Small Schools Team of the Year and Coach Kari Jung was named the CBS MaxPreps Small Schools Coach of the Year.

Jung said shortly after the season ended the emphasis was on daily improvement more than winning.

"As a coach, I don't go into the season thinking, 'Let's try to win every set.' Your ultimate goal is to try to get better each match," Jung said at the time. "Things just fell into place for us. We're just very fortunate that we didn't have injuries and illnesses." (American News, Dec. 13, 2012)

Again, another successful coach who won more than anybody else that season, without a huge emphasis on winning. It is a method that works.

It's a system that works as Jung has had numerous players that have gone on to experience success at the college level.

Now just because you do the little things correct, it does not mean you are destined to win a state championship. However, it is difficult to win a state title without doing those. More importantly, by doing those little things it will allow your team to reach its full potential and therefore be more successful. Again, winning state titles cannot be the measuring stick, because if it is, we know 99 percent of the teams will not measure up.

It's interesting, because while it takes a fair of amount of talent to have a competitive squad year in and year out, there is also another constant in that equation and it is stability in the coaching ranks. There is simply no way some of the small communities in South Dakota have the best athletes every year. Yet each season there are certain programs that are always among the state's elite. The common denominator: each has a coach that is knowledgeable, passionate, gets the most out of the athletes and has years of experience with the program.

In addition to the aforementioned Warner volleyball and Ipswich cross-country and track and field squads, some of those small-town programs which always seem to be among the finest in the state each year and their coach include Bridgewater-Emery/Ethan football (Jeff VanLeur), Avon football (Tom Culver), Northwestern volleyball (Nora Groft), Sully Buttes girls' basketball (Mark Senftner), Langford Area boys' basketball (Paul Raasch), Corsica-Stickney boys' basketball (Mike Tuschen), White River boys' basketball (Eldon Marshall), Clark-Willow Lake boys' basketball (Jerome Nesheim), Faulkton wrestling (Shane Geditz), and Webster wrestling (Wade Rausch) just to name a few.

While many coaches pour everything they have into their athletes, there is also a disturbing element at work. Despite fielding competitive teams on a regular basis, some of my coaching friends have told me it can still be a rough go with some of the parents. I know of at least two examples of coaches who have won state championships who have gotten anonymous letters telling them how they are ruining their programs. Seriously?

If that's the case with quality coaches who have proven track records, I shudder to think what life is like for those coaches who struggle to win contests.

While some parents hide behind anonymous letters, others are much more emboldened to have their opinions heard.

About a dozen years ago, a group of parents filed a lawsuit against a school board because they disagreed with the school's basketball coach over issues of playing time and substitution patterns.

It gets much worse than that, though. I once talked to a coach who told me he received a death threat from a parent. Simply unbelievable and a sad commentary on what we have become as a society. And all over games that kids play.

I wish I could say things are getting better, but they are getting worse. Within the past year, I know of two coaches who were run out of programs because of parents. And I'm sure you can recall a couple of brawls between parents that broke out at youth sporting events that gained national attention.

Some parents are far more determined to achieve what they believe to be success than the athletes and coaches. That is a major problem.

I covered a girls' basketball game once and noticed a woman having a small meltdown not far from me. Her daughter's team happened to be winning the game and playing very well. I was curious as to her demeanor before realizing she was throwing a fit because her daughter was on the bench and not getting the playing time the mother felt she deserved. It did not take long before even the fans of that team started inching away from her in the stands.

I also heard of another incident at a welcome home celebration for a state championship football squad. As the fans filtered in and congratulated the squad on the accomplishment, a parent said to the coach, "Congratulations. I thought my son should have played more, but congratulations."

So, what is it parents really want, besides more than what they deserve?

In a perfect world, do parents want an undefeated season, capped by a state championship, with their son or daughter being the star player, making all the big plays at the end of games, and then receiving all of the major postseason awards available? Imagine if that was every single parent's desire? How is a coach supposed to be able to work in that kind of environment?

I totally understand not all coaches are top of the line, but neither are all of the athletes, but that does nothing to quiet the critics. A few coaches have told me they shouldn't have any problem understanding how to coach, because many people sitting in the stands tell them how they should do it. Again, it really comes down to understanding roles.

When coaches coach, players play and parents and fans support the athletes in a positive manner, things tend to go much better than when roles are switched.

20

JOY IN THE JOURNEY

It's not just about working hard, it's about working together.
You have to care more about the team than you do about yourself.
—John Calipari

There are different philosophies when it comes to parents watching their kids participate in extra-curricular activities. Some can't miss a thing, some don't have a desire to attend much of anything, and some manage to get to what they can because of jobs, finances, etc.

I was one of those parents who never wanted to miss anything. Whether it was because my parents never missed an event of mine or because I missed so many of our kids' birthdays or because I knew the window to watch our son and daughter was very small and wouldn't stay open for long, I wanted to get to every game, concert and speech meet possible. And through understanding employers, I pretty much did. I basically had the philosophy you can always make money, but you can't always make a memory.

Because both of our children were born in mid-November, I missed countless birthdays as I was busy covering state tournaments. We simply celebrated before I left or after I came back. However, I can count on about two fingers the other events I missed during their school days.

I will admit, I have wondered if my presence did put undue pressure on our kids. However, I also knew I did not want to miss out on any of their significant milestones. Looking back on it, I am not one bit sorry I tried to get to every event possible.

I was at the gym in Mellette when Mariah found out after a JV match she was suiting up for varsity that evening for the first time ever. Seeing her pure jubilation in that moment was priceless. I was there on the campus of the South Dakota School of Mines in Rapid City when she competed in the State Geography contest. I was at The Huether Family Match Pointe tennis center in Sioux Falls when Isaiah won the consolation championship, becoming the first Roncalli player in more than a decade to make the podium at top flight singles. I was at Courtside Plus Fitness Center in Fargo, North Dakota when he defeated players from North Dakota, Minnesota and Wisconsin to win the boys' 16 singles championship. No, I don't regret being there to witness those events at all.

It's interesting, because as much as teenage kids act like they don't want to be around their parents, in reality most are longing for support and attention. Throughout the past two seasons of the Legends Sports Show, I have found out why various athletes chose the colleges they eventually attended. I don't think it's a coincidence two of the most accomplished athletes in the history of Northern State decided to play for the Wolves because of ties to their parents.

Scott Bosanko, who some consider to be the greatest basketball player in Aberdeen history, had a phenomenal career and finished as Northern's all-time leading scorer at the time. Bosanko, who was selected by the Dallas Mavericks in the 1981 NBA draft, told me he had opportunities to play at other places, but decided to remain in town in large part so that his parents (who never missed high school game) could continue to watch him play.

"I was heavily recruited. Sometimes you get letters from all these colleges and you're not really sure if they're very interested in you or if they just send out letters, but I had lots of offers from inside the state of South Dakota. And probably the main reason that I stayed in Aberdeen was, one the Civic Arena, but probably most importantly is that I was going to get to play in front of my mom and dad for the next four years." (The Legends Sports Show, Feb. 22, 2018)

Meanwhile, Rich Andrzjewski, who hailed from Arlington, said he came to Northern because of his mom. "Andy" could have gone to numerous other places, but had the career of a lifetime for the Wolves. He lettered in football, basketball, baseball and track and field all four years. His 16 letters gained him national acclaim from the likes of Sports Illustrated and Paul Harvey. He told me his family situation factored into his decision to remain in the area.

"I had opportunities to go to a lot of different schools, some bigger schools, a lot of the schools in South Dakota, virtually all of the schools in South Dakota. But my father passed away when I was a junior in high school and my mother asked me to do one thing and that was to stay close enough to home that she could come and watch me play. So that's why I stayed in South Dakota." (The Legends Sports Show, Feb. 2, 2017).

Now, I totally get there are various reasons why individuals select the colleges they do. Some want a specific degree, some receive scholarships they can't pass up, and some just can't wait to leave home. Yet, there is no denying the impact a positive parent-child relationship can have. And I know of numerous examples where children have left home and the parents have driven hundreds of miles to make sure they never miss a contest.

While I have enjoyed watching our kids perform in various activities through the years, I will never forget the significance of the journey itself. From Rosholt to Rapid City, from Herreid to Harrisburg, there have been so many memorable moments along the way.

For starters, there were all of the unique concession stands, including one in a basement at Herreid. And of course, the selections along the way were nothing short of stellar as recapped in one of my blogs.

"In my opinion, there is no concession stand that offers more variety than the one at Sunshine Bible Academy. From chili and walking tacos, to soft serve ice cream and expresso drinks, the SBA stand could go into business as a small restaurant. The food is very reasonable, very good and very memorable.

Of course, some schools offer food through fundraising groups that may not always be a part of the regular concession menu. I find it fascinating that certain schools offer food that matches up with their particular culture.

For instance, at games that I have attended in Eureka, knoephla soup is one of the items that is available. That is very fitting for a German community.

This past week, I attended a game in Waubay, which has numerous Native American students. I found myself eating frybread with Wojapi sauce (something I relate to blueberry syrup). I had never even heard of that, let alone tried it. Simply delicious." (Are we On? Dave Vilhauer blog, Feb. 3, 2017)

Then there were all of the gyms I got a chance to visit, each unique in its own way. I will always remember the historic Community Hall in Summit, which was built in 1953. A player could literally stand out of bounds, inbound the ball with one hand and grab a popcorn from the concession stand with the other without moving at all.

And at each locale there were friendships to rekindle and new acquaintances to make. Some of the best people I have encountered in life were met during the course of sporting events.

Sure, each step of the way I was there to support our children, but I can honestly say that on most occasions, I can't really remember how many points or aces they had or if Aberdeen Christian even won for that matter. While I thoroughly enjoyed being a proud parent in the stands, to fully appreciate the joy of the parenting experience you really need to take in all of the people, places and things.

21

THE FINISH LINE

Plays are not as important as players, and players
are not as important as teammates.
—Don Meyer

I have had the opportunity to interview many former athletes who are now parents of athletes. When I ask them to compare the difference between playing and watching, nearly all of them say it's much more difficult sitting in the stands because they have no control over what is happening on the field or on the court. It can truly be a helpless feeling.

Helpless may be the best way to describe a good share of my son's final high school tennis season. Through a variety of circumstances, nearly half of the season was wiped out. Weather conditions claimed many of the matches, scheduling glitches took a few more and before you knew it, a total of 13 matches had been cancelled. What was supposed to be one of Roncalli's best tennis teams in years turned into one of the most frustrating seasons in recent memory.

As a parent of a senior player, it was tough to swallow and as a tennis advocate, it was mind-boggling to see how none of the matches got rescheduled, knowing that would have never been the case in any other sport.

One beautiful day after another passed by without hardly any matches being played, and it dawned on me the opportunity to watch Isaiah play was evaporating faster than what I expected. I finally came to the realization I was just going to have to savor every moment I could, because the finish line was coming a lot quicker than what I wanted or anticipated.

As I head down to Sioux Falls for the final regular season matches, it occurs to me I have made this trek many times in six years of Roncalli tennis and this will be the final one. By my calculations this is my 42nd overall trip to watch high school tennis with the final one coming next week at the state tournament in Rapid City. I wonder what my emotions will be like knowing this is the last hurrah.

In what has become the norm through the years, the weather is cold, damp and windy for the matches in Sioux Falls. As we walk into McKennan Park on Saturday morning, a unique feeling comes over me. I realize this is the location where Isaiah played his first ever varsity match six years ago and also won his first ever varsity match later that season. It's almost like saying goodbye to a longtime friend. Now I'm really wondering how I will handle next week's state tourney, because regardless of the results, it will mark the end of being the parent of a high school athlete.

Having watched six straight years of tennis, I can tell you every top player from every school. I know that Isaiah has a tough draw at his final state tournament. If he wins his first match he will face a player from Rapid City Stevens he has already lost to twice before this season. I also know no matter how you slice it, there are a lot of quality players in first flight singles so there really are no easy matches for anyone.

Playing number one, you are always facing a school's best player and I have come to realize through the years just about every team has at least one standout player. As I like to say about playing in the top flight, "It's a tough way to make a living."

Isaiah wins his first match and now faces Jamison Pfingston of Stevens. I know it will be an uphill battle, although in the two previous matches Isaiah has had some chances.

Pfingston dominates the first set, winning 6-0. I am doing a slow boil. I get up from my chair and decide to walk around and check out a few other matches, all the while keeping an eye on my son.

I'm not sure if my leaving has anything to do with it, but soon Isaiah gets his teeth into the match. To his credit, he changes strategy and changes his fortunes. The second set is tight the whole way and Isaiah pulls out a victory to force a super-tiebreaker for the third set. OK, now I am officially nervous.

The winner of this match will advance to the quarterfinals, the loser is headed to the consolation round. There is nothing I can say or do that will impact the outcome. Talk about a helpless feeling.

(There are times you have no control over the parent trapped within).

Pfingston comes up clutch on a couple of key points and claims the victory. While I am disappointed, I am also pleased by how Isaiah competed, especially after that first set.

Following the match, it is apparent Isaiah is stung by the result. He is taking it harder than me, which is exactly how it should be. (Remember the parent should never want it worse than the athlete).

I know we still have doubles and consolation singles remaining so there is still plenty of tennis left. Isaiah and his partner, Lucas Goetz, suffer a loss in doubles, but also win a consolation match. As the day ends, the players are tired, hungry and glad the opening day is finished.

A group of parents decide to carry on a Roncalli tennis tradition. We head to Rockerville. It is an out of the way location on the way to Mount Rushmore. Rockerville is so small, it is not even listed among the South Dakota towns. However, it is home to a restaurant called the Gaslight, a place we have visited every year for the past five seasons.

Our table is lively as usual. It includes Ron and Amy Hellwig, Lee and Peg Goetz, John and Stacy Kokales in addition to Lauretta and I. Rod and Michele

Titus were unable to join us. These Roncalli parents have become like family. They are some of the most genuine people I have ever met.

On this particular night, there is a storm waging outside with thunder, lighting and rain. There is also a storm waging inside of me as I ponder what might be Isaiah's final day of high school tennis the next day. I know Isaiah has winnable matches, but I also know he will have to play some of his best tennis of the season to be able to make it Saturday's final round.

As I contemplate how I will handle my emotions during the next 24 hours, it occurs to me what I will truly miss is being around these Roncalli tennis parents. We have shared so many laughs and good times through the years and it seems like somebody always has a birthday to celebrate.

There are so many memories connected to these tennis parents. No matter where he sits, John Kokales is always at the head of the table. It was at the Gaslight two years ago I actually floated the idea of writing a book to Lee Goetz. The gals not only have been instrumental in lining up rides, they also laugh at my corny jokes. It's a fact that no matter what happens on the tennis court, this promises to be a tough weekend knowing this type of fellowship will come to a close.

Through the years I have managed to shoot a variety of photos and videos just for keepsakes more than anything. There are times when Isaiah is not particularly fond of it and there are times when I wonder what other parents think of me while I'm doing that. Do they think I am one of "those parents?"

However, during the state tourney, I notice a variety of parents doing the exact same thing, especially parents of senior players. They are equipped with phones and cameras trying to capture one final moment. Suddenly I don't feel so out of place.

Isaiah wins his first match on Friday morning before we get news he has just won the Dr. Harold E. Salem Christian Character Award at Aberdeen Christian's awards program back home. This is the highest honor the school hands out, named after a wonderful man of God and a close family friend. To me, it feels like Isaiah has just won a state championship.

Isaiah wins his second match and then has to face a difficult foe who was upset in the opening round of the tourney. I know this could be the end of the road for singles. Unlike last year when Isaiah came back to win the consolation championship, he comes up short this time around.

A short while later he plays a doubles match where he and Lucas Goetz are eliminated meaning Isaiah's career is over. I am not even sure how to react. It seems just like yesterday when I was in Brandon on that sunny Friday afternoon six years ago watching his first state tourney and now it's all over.

While I am disappointed to see it end this way, I know the impact he has made on this program. He has become the first boys' player in Roncalli history to spend four years at number one singles. He has won more than 100 combined singles and doubles matches during his career and medaled in both singles and doubles. He has won multiple matches in six different state tournaments. There is nothing to feel bad about.

Saturday is a big day for the Cavaliers. They still have a chance to win state championships at a couple of flights and have an outside shot at placing in the top six in team points, which means a place on the podium and a plaque (which would be a major accomplishment for the second smallest school in South Dakota to offer tennis).

Isaiah is no longer playing but fulfills his role as a leader offering encouragement to his teammates. The race for sixth as a team is going to be tight between Roncalli and Sioux Falls Washington. The Cavaliers win a fair share of matches and put a fitting end on their season when Colton Hellwig and Spencer Titus cap an undefeated season by winning the state championship at third flight doubles. There are smiles all around.

As we pack up our gear and get ready to head to the awards area, it appears Washington will finish sixth and Roncalli one spot away from making the podium. There are no regrets knowing everybody did what they could.

Assistant coach Ron Meier and I are glancing at the final results when Ron notices a mistake. It shows Roncalli losing a match it had won. I tell him to inform the tournament officials but doubt they gave the team points to the wrong team.

In the meantime, workers find another error, this one giving Washington a win that belonged to an opponent. When the two errors are fixed, it propels Roncalli into sixth place by a mere one and half points.

While the coaches know the situation, the players do not so when the awards are announced, there is a surprised and satisfied group of Roncalli tennis players who take the podium. And there on the top rung with plaque in hand is Isaiah Vilhauer. This is a very good way to end a memorable career.

As I walk back to the vehicle, I pass Roger Damgaard of Sioux Falls, a grandparent of one of the Sioux Falls O'Gorman players. He says to me, "Congratulations, you are now officially retired."

I stop in my tracks, thinking, wait a minute, I still have quite a few years left before I can stop working. It then dawns on me he meant I am officially retired as a parent of an athlete. I smile and say, "That's right. Thank you."

It is already getting late, we have a nearly six-hour drive ahead of us and there is graduation the next day. I am too preoccupied to feel much of anything at the moment.

Isaiah, like his sister, Mariah three years before, is the student speaker at graduation. He also leads two praise and worship songs. Reality is setting in that this chapter of his life and also of my life has come to a close and looking back on it, I wouldn't have changed a thing.

I'm really not sure what it will be like going to games in the future. Sports have always been a big part of my life and I definitely don't see that changing regardless of who is in uniform. I am just grateful I have gotten the opportunities to be a part of something special. Parents, don't take these years for granted. They promise to be the most emotional, stress-filled, unpredictable, joyous, meaningful and rewarding times of your life.

22

LEGACY

'Coach' is one of the greatest titles anybody can have.
They impact kids' lives in a way that no other teacher does.
—Phil Knight

The vast majority of us are not going to be parents of professional athletes. In fact, most of us are not even going to be parents of college athletes. So, what is your measure of success going to be when it comes to your son or daughter?

I can tell you right now, if it has anything to do with state championships, wins or personal statistics, prepare yourself for disappointment and heartache, because there's a good chance your son or daughter will never be able to do enough to meet your unrealistic expectations. Nor should that even be their goal. Remember, this is their own personal journey, not yours.

I have always tried to never lose sight of the fact extra-curricular activities, and sports in general, are really for the athletes. While they provide entertainment, a diversion, a source of school pride, and sometimes even an identity for a small town itself, at the end of the day, it is what it is, games played by teenage kids who are learning a variety of valuable life lessons.

For that reason alone, I have done my best to always give a voice to the athletes involved. While I enjoy interviewing coaches, I also am intentional about interviewing the individuals who compete. When I was at the paper,

I always had a rule of thumb to interview at least one and sometimes two athletes at every game I covered. When it came to football, I would make sure to interview at least one lineman, a person who seldom gets attention, but who is vital to team success nonetheless.

Now that I am in radio, the same principles apply. I have two high school radio shows and I interview at least two athletes on a weekly basis. Some handle the attention better than others, but each has a special story to share and all are worthy of the spotlight regardless of position or statistics.

I understand coaches are the leaders and I interview them as well, but sometimes we tend to forget about the athletes, especially those who may not get the credit they deserve because they aren't the ones racking up the kills, yards or points.

I love the athletes who are low-key, and go out and perform without drawing attention to themselves. I'd rather watch a silent-assassin who drills a dagger jump shot like it's routine than a kid who has to make a spectacle of himself after every single shot. In fact, I have a hard time watching guys who make it all about themselves.

I totally get the benefits of playing with emotion. In fact, sometimes it's hard to be on top of your game without some positive energy. However, we have totally crossed the line when it comes to what is acceptable behavior, especially at the high school level. I cringe every time I see a player make a 3-pointer and then use his hands to blow smoke rings, shoot imaginary pistols, spread his arms in a flying motion going down the court, etc. You know the type of gestures I am talking about.

You show me coaches who allow those type of antics and I will show you coaches who are some of the least respected by their peers, not to mention opposing parents and fans. The same thing goes when it comes to disrespecting officials. Once players begin questioning calls, a coach's reputation will soon come into question as well. I've even seen athletes argue calls in summer league games. Really?

And I can't imagine a single parent who can be pleased with that kind of attitude coming from a son or a daughter.

So where did we ever get the idea showboating, taunting and questioning authority was ever an acceptable practice in the first place? It doesn't take much to connect the dots. Kids tend to model the behavior of their favorite athletes. Unfortunately, some of those professional athletes (you pick the sport), do not always exhibit the best judgement. While parents and coaches can't do much about a star athlete's antics, they can and should be able to have a great impact on the behavior of a high school athlete. Again, we have to practice what we preach.

The late Don Meyer who I had the privilege to work with when he was the men's basketball coach at Northern State, perhaps put it best when he said, "It is foolish to expect a young man to follow your advice and to ignore your example."

Coaches and parents, do your best to model the right kinds of actions. And athletes, don't make it about yourselves. Everybody should do their best to display class and character.

I don't pretend to have all of the answers. I have never coached an organized game in my life. I realize all of the demands, pressures and expectations put on coaches today. We live in a time where we often fire good teachers who are marginal coaches, and sometimes hire good coaches who are marginal teachers. Our priorities are getting more warped by the day.

Still, coaches please understand the significant role you are playing in the lives of impressionable teenage kids. The late Rev. Billy Graham said, "A coach will impact more people in one year than the average person will in an entire lifetime." Let that sink in a for a minute.

Don't make it all about winning and losing, and definitely don't make it about your agenda or building a personal resume. If your love for teaching kids and passion for helping them to develop into the best well-rounded individuals they can be isn't first and foremost in your profession, it's probably time to do something else. No matter how much society may say otherwise, it simply cannot be about titles won and overall winning percentage.

And now a word or two about being a sports parent from what I have discovered through the years.

High school sports are not about you. It is not about the title you never won. It is not about carrying on a family tradition. It is not about how you will be viewed in the community. You cannot want it more than your athlete. Period. Exclamation point.

There are definite roles for being a parent and you should never feel your role is insignificant. By the same token, never overestimate your role, either.

Be there for your son or daughter. One of the worst things you can do is show a total lack of interest.

Provide an atmosphere of confidence and never give up on your child. Don't discourage your athlete by telling them they'll never be good enough or by pointing out all of the things they are doing wrong. While your constructive criticism may be well intentioned, most kids don't want to hear about all of their mistakes. In fact, words of praise will do much more for a person than you can ever imagine (coaches take note).

Lend a listening ear. Allow your son or daughter to share the joys and frustrations of athletic events without letting your own opinions take over the conversation.

Understand that ultimately you are not responsible for your child's happiness. This is a difficult one to comprehend. From the time your children are born, you want to provide the best possible environment for them to grow up in. Parents love to see their kids be happy. However, there comes a time when you cannot always be there for them and ensure their happiness. If you are feeling responsible for their success and happiness in athletics bad things will eventually happen. You will be tempted to "pull a few strings" to make sure they are happy or you will likely feel a great deal of personal guilt if your child doesn't have a good experience. And who knows, you may be the parent of a child who will never be happy no matter what you do. Just be there to support and encourage every step of the way.

Don't embarrass your son or daughter at games. When people are watching you in the stands more than your athlete on the court, that is a sign of a major problem.

Don't panic when (not if) adversity strikes. It's just a matter of time before something doesn't go your child's way. It could be losing a starting role, it could be a game-costing blunder or it could be an injury. Let your son or daughter work through it, because it will serve as a good lesson on how to handle situations when things go awry later in life. (And who knows, it could just turn out to be a blessing in disguise like it was for Isaiah).

Don't make life miserable for the coach. If there is an issue, have your child talk to the coach, because it is his or her coach, not yours. And while it may be extremely difficult, don't disrespect the coach in the presence of your son or daughter. This will plant seeds of doubt in the athlete's mind about leadership and potentially destroy team unity. This same principle applies when talking about other players on the team as well.

Always place team success ahead of individual achievement. I believe if all parents were able to accomplish this one key component it could change nearly the entire dynamic of today's sport culture. Notice I did not say winning. Team success is getting a group of individuals to bond into something much bigger than themselves to accomplish something they could never do on their own.

And never think you are too old to learn. I have always maintained there are so many life-lessons to be learned through athletics, things like self-discipline, learning to work with others, finding ways to deal with adversity, pushing yourself to find true potential, among many others. What I failed to understand is there are also so many life-lessons for parents to be learned through athletics.

Being a parent challenges you to show self-control, maintain proper perspective, value the journey more than the results. Lessons are there for the taking if we will take a step away from the competition and understand what is really important.

There were two prime examples of lessons to be learned in the spring of 2018 in South Dakota, both involving individuals from Sioux Falls and both of which drew national attention. One of them took place at the State Boys' Tennis Tournament in Rapid City where a coach and parent from Sioux Falls O'Gorman filed a lawsuit against the South Dakota High School Activities Association after they did not like a ruling enforced by the SDSHAA for being late to a match. That ruling resulted in the forfeiture of a match for a top-seeded doubles team.

The other example took place at the State A Girls' Golf Tournament in Dell Rapids. Defending state champion Kate Wynja of Sioux Falls Christian appeared to have defended her individual state title, only to realize following the tourney that she had inadvertently signed an incorrect scorecard. Upon realizing the error, she self-reported her mistake. That error resulted in her being disqualified and her team missing out on a state team championship as well.

Two very different examples which will likely be talked about for years to come, both with valuable lessons if we are paying attention.

In addition to a pair of high school shows, I also host a weekly program called the Legends Sports Show and have interviewed some of the most decorated athletes in state history. One of the questions I ask of each one is what life-long lessons did you learn from athletics you were able to use throughout your entire career? Not a single person has talked about the ability to win, records obtained or personal fame. Imagine that.

Sports really aren't all about winning or losing. If you don't believe that, just ask somebody who has recorded great accomplishments in the game.

Again, I applaud all of the coaches, athletes and parents who combine to provide a setting in which so many positives can transpire. I truly believe the best leaders in our country have had and will continue to have a background in extra-curricular activities. There is no substitute for being a part of something much bigger than ourselves.

The next time you are at a game, understand the players involved are likely the future leaders of our country. Encourage them, motivate them, challenge them and above all support them. If everybody knows their roles and carries them out, we can all be successful regardless of the final score.

As you finish reading this book, some of you may think that I am writing specifically about you, but I'm not. Far more of you will think that I am not writing specifically about you, but I am. In either case, always respect the game, support your children to the best of your ability and handle every situation with character and class. That is the best way to handle the parent trapped within.

ACKNOWLEDGEMENTS

There are so many people who have helped to make *The Parent Trapped Within* become a reality.

First and foremost, I want to thank my Lord and Savior Jesus Christ. I truly believe that this book is God-inspired and all glory should go to Him.

A big thank you to my family members: my wife Lauretta, son Isaiah, and daughter Mariah. Not only have they provided plenty of material for this book, but they have been there to encourage, challenge and motivate me each step of the way.

A huge shout out to some of my former colleagues at the American News. Ryan Deal and John Papendick are good friends and two of the most respected journalists in South Dakota. Their editing skills helped to advance the book and make it what it is. John Davis is the best sports photographer in the business. His work adorns the cover of this book. Also, a big thanks to Mariah for her photoshop skills that added a new dimension to the cover.

Also, I owe a huge debt of gratitude to Buster Olney for his foreword to the book. Buster is a great guy who has a wonderful sense of perspective in today's sports world. Also, a big thank you to Dave Goren, Jo Auch, Eddie Timanus and Holly Hoffman for their reviews of the book. I have gotten to know each of these individuals on a personal level, and I appreciate their knowledge and perspective when it comes to sports.

A special thank you to friends Carmen Meyer, Jerry and Sharon Stroh, Tom Gross and Tom Young for their words of wisdom and faith in helping me to complete the task.

Of course, I could not have written this book without all of the coaches, parents and athletes who I have had the privilege to cover in nearly four decades of my life. You have provided so many memorable moments and it is my desire that *The Parent Trapped Within* will give something back to each person who has played a positive role in the world of athletics.

God bless and enjoy the book.

ABOUT THE AUTHOR

Dave Vilhauer is in his 39th year as a member of the media. He worked at the Aberdeen American News for nearly 36 years. He began writing game stories for the paper as a junior in high school and later served as assistant sports editor. He joined Hub City Radio in the summer of 2016 where he currently serves as the News and Sports Information Director. In addition to writing a weekly blog (Are we On?), he also hosts three sports shows that he created (Inside the LRC, Inside the NEC, and the Legends Sports Show).

He has interviewed numerous national sports figures including Michael Jordan, Richard Petty, Kirby Puckett, Bill Self, and John Wooden.

He has covered a variety of sporting events featuring nearly 150 state tournaments and meets, 72 state championship games (including a stretch of 21 consecutive State B boys' basketball championship contests), in addition to a national championship.

He was selected the South Dakota Sports Writer of the Year by the South Dakota High School Coaches Association in 2002, and by the National Sportscasters and Sportswriters Association (now the National Sports Media Association) in 2008. He was chosen the Press Person of the Year by the South Dakota Wrestling Coaches Association in 1993, 1997 and 1998. He received the Distinguished Service Award from the South Dakota High School Activities Association in 2013. He most recently won an Eric Sevareid Award of Merit for one of his radio shows selected by the Midwest Broadcast Journalists Association.

He lives in Aberdeen, S.D. He can be found on Twitter @DaveVilhauer and also on Facebook. To find out more about this book or share a thought, please visit *www.theparenttrappedwithin.com*.